A Flanshaw Tale 1974-1
Dedicated to My Daugh
Beautiful Mum and Nan

Contents

Introduction 2

Acknowledgements

Thanks to Kate for her help and the suggestion she gave me many months ago in starting a blog without her this book would never have happened.

Also to my friends past and present who have given me encouragement along the way Thank you

Introduction

I've never written anything before in my life this is my first stab at writing I hope I don't let you down please be aware though unlike most books that try to speak the queens own, I occasionally say something the way I speak. I call it Flanshaw talk so bear with it if you come across it. Well, this book what can I say its something I have wanted to do for as long as I can remember my childhood had many great moments and growing up on Flanshaw gifted me some of the best moments of my life the mid-'70s were a great time to be alive as a kid. We made our own fun! we made fun out of nothing ! its cost us nowt and that pleased our parents as well no doubt it was a situation which was pretty much win-win for all concerned. And on these pages your about to read I want to try and get across you, the reader a picture of life on a council estate through two decades the '70s and the 80's I know for most this won't be too hard as most of you will have grown up same as me I speak a lot of my childhood but i,m pretty sure I speak of yours too, that is my goal to take you on a journey home I know this introduction could be much longer than it is but I don't like to ramble on too much.

These days I suffer From Rheumatoid Arthritis - more good days than bad mostly due to a strong mentality I have developed over the years by reading lots of personal development etc ... my condition has nothing to do with the years of punching and kicking in my dojo's or the training in Kumite (sparring) unfortunately for me, it's a hereditary issue passed down to me by my mum, an unavoidable thing really, so these days I simply cannot train in or teach Martial Arts anymore something I really enjoyed, was helping others achieve their goals, helping people young and old, some with learning difficulties and some without. Some with Physical disabilities and again some without I had no set criteria in my classes only the will to try your best I helped many families, mostly children, but also, mums and dads, some suffered adhd some needed confidence many other things too martial arts have many great benefits from physical fitness, to mental and physical coordination, motivation, giving my students goals to reach etc. there all life skills aren't they.?

And I was paid handsomely although the Money was always the byproduct of what I did, the buzz for me was in watching my students grow in confidence seeing them make new friends that were my payday. I'm not and have never been materialistic.

So anyway, unfortunately, I cannot do any of the above anymore, so I got to thinking …. "How can I give people enjoyment the way I did in my Martial Arts Days?" and the one thing I always wanted to do is get down on paper my childhood - my Life Story, if you will? Sometimes humorous occasionally sad, I write it as clear as I can, whatever is in my head I shall write on these pages, so, bear with me, and I hope in my heart you will get as much enjoyment from this as I did writing it. It's based on my childhood in the mid-'70s and throughout the '80s growing up on Flanshaw, A council estate in the heart of Wakefield. What was then a tight-knit community with all kinds of characters It starts at my tender age of 6 up to my ripe old age 20, it's my childhood but I truly believe it is also yours too?

So, onto my reason

I believe anything we do in life if we attack it with a big enough reason, it can be achieved - as long as we don't bog ourselves down in the 'how to achieve it'. How is important of course but in all honesty, a tad boring? I prefer the 'WHY'. A 'WHY' is stronger than a 'HOW'.

A 'HOW' is how to achieve something I already know what I want to achieve, so why focus on it? Boring, right?

To focus on the 'HOW' I seriously would, in all honesty, give up writing this book before I even start out of sheer boredom if nothing else. Whereas, a 'WHY' will burn a fire in you. Something I was taught pretty much from day one training in the Dojo. I used it throughout my time in the Martial Arts and to this day and in my life when things get tough wherever possible really.

So, my reason? My 'WHY' well it's to simply pass my story down to my beautiful daughter and to my future grandkids - my whole life as I remember it, so she can too safe in the Knowledge pass my Tale on through the future generations of our family when I'm dead and buried. To put it simply I don't want the childhood I was fortunate to have had, ever be forgotten

A legacy if you will?

So, to all my old friend's past and present where shall, we start?
How about the beginning shall we?

Chapter One

Beginnings

January 1974, New Year's Day, my beautiful Nan passed away in her sleep
after reading me and my siblings a bedtime story, Jack and the Beanstalk,
and another about a woman who had to go away and leave her children
for a while but whilst absent she would send them gifts and sweets and all
things they loved most every day with a letter for them all.

Looking back, I now know that story was made up by my Nan I was also
told years later by mum she knew she was dying and her wish was to be
with us all to the end. It devastated my mum absolutely crushed her, my
siblings and me as we were not used to death, nor was mum having lost
her dad many years before I didn't know at the time why people had to
die, especially the kind ones like my Nan. It was wrong I remember sitting
downstairs in the room playing with my action man Santa had brought
me the week previous I sat there on our well-worn carpet not even
wanting to play with my favourite toy, I was just thinking of Nan and
asking myself why she was still asleep? she always got up early to make
our breakfasts.

I was not allowed to go upstairs where she lay at rest. It was all so
confusing as I couldn't understand why I was not allowed to see her, she
always had time for us did my Nan. Any time of the day and whatever she
was doing in the day, housework, cooking, washing up etc. she would
always have time to pick me or my siblings up and give us a hug she
would always ask "so how many bags of sugar do you love me then?", my

answer was always "all the bags of sugar in the world Nan". She would then kiss me softly on the cheek and place me back down on the floor. "Well run along then and go play out just make sure you behave for your mum today love" she would say

When the harsh reality hit home she had died It ripped me apart, as it did my mum who was left to look after us all by herself and in Seventies Britain and being a single parent, this was quite a task believe me.

I respect the way my mum over the years for the way she fought tooth and nail to bring all six of us up on her own the way she did. she once even gathered us all around her you know and asked us what we thought of the idea if she ever wanted to get married – "No Mum", and she agreed on no questions. Looking back on that it was I guess a tad selfish but we were too young to ever remember having a dad so we did not know what a difference in mum's life that may have made, anyway, Mum being Mum she went along with our wishes and sacrificed her own happiness for us all. All the life she gave of herself and gave us small treats whenever she could, and even still, to this day she now gives us all £50 quid every few months, I once asked her why? And she replied: "Well you never had anything as kids, did you?" So, our old house stood on Wilson Terrace Thornes on a street that used to be next to what is now the former Jolly Sailor Inn 1971 - 1974 it was a rundown old house was ours but it was filled with so much love

I remember we had a

A coal yard opposite our garden called Bells it supplied coal to most of Wakefield. And In the winter, I would often walk out of our garden tread on the deep snow, often up to my knees, just to fill a carrier bag with coal for my mum and Nan, it conveniently fell under the perimeter fence this happened regularly as old Belly had so much of the black stuff it would often spill under his fence.

We had free coal most the time and on those nights when the sky was full of snow and remembering the smells of burning coal in the air, spewing from just the four houses on our streets chimneys it was a magical time to be alive, less is more as they say and living on Wilson terrace was proof of that. So basically, we moved from there around May 1974. Our street was up for demolition by the local corporation and so we made a move to a new house to a place called Flanshaw in Wakefield it seemed at the time a million miles from Thornes. I remember moving in a rusty, dusty old Naylor's removal wagon that used to be based on Northgate, Wakefield,

opposite the place, the less well-off folk get married. Anyway turns out we got a discount cos my brother worked there and, sitting on that old mattress Nan had died on months earlier because money was tight and mum couldn't afford a new one so myself together along with my siblings rode the journey to our new home.

Whilst sat there all that went through my mind was that I was going on an adventure, and looking out the rear as we rode along I just remember seeing fluffy white clouds rolling by. And whilst sitting there a feeling of excitement and anticipation, then emotions overcame me as began to think of Nan again and the happy times she gave me and as fantastic and loving as the times that they were at Wilson terrace experiencing Nans love and listening intently to her bedtime stories, then next morning waking up to deep snow on the ground Christmas morning and playing out etc, and in the summertime the sailing on those home-made rafts on the Frog Pond under those 99 archers at back of us. I never realised and, how would I? of how much of an adventure I was about to experience or even what lay ahead in my life. Mix all that up and thoughts whizzing through my head of missing my Nan I was at that point suddenly distracted

As the removal van suddenly screeched to a halt, the brake noises slowly faded as the scruffy looking man with a flat cap who had driven us there opened the half-shut shutters of his wagon, A warm sunny day greeted me, children, pretty scary children in my mind, dressed in flares - girls shouting and running around in the street skipping, boys riding their Tomahawk Budgie and chopper bikes, popping wheelies, riding past me at quite a speed. Girls playing with their Cindy dolls crawling in and out of their plastic Wendy houses on their front lawns, making what looked like pretending cups of tea with colourful plastic cups and saucers. There Neatly dressed, and proud, mums talking over the garden gate to neighbours, dads mowing their lawns under the summer sun and that particular day a cloudless blue sky.

I sensed this was going to be quite an adventure!

You have to understand at this point that I had come from a pretty much-sheltered upbringing, the only friends I had up until the age of 6 were my siblings to play with. So, to suddenly see this world away from Thornes - was a real eye opener if I'm honest and a touch scary an all.

Rows upon rows of houses all stuck together in lumps of 2 they were. Our old street only had four houses, suddenly I felt nervous for the first time in my life.

However, I did, make friends but it took me a long time. I got to know some good friends on Keswick Drive there was Gavin, also his brother Michael, they lived to the left of the ginnel opposite our house. Then there was Mick Charlesworth who was always riding along at speed, showing off, riding past me his bum raised off the seat of his Chopper speeding along like he was Barry Sheene. He had a sister too called Lisa, Lisa had a friend next door to her called Michelle a lovely looking girl who just so happened became my brother Mick's first girlfriend, and then there was Sue Heslop who lived the same side as me but four doors down she was a right character too and many others too which I will get to later in my tale, anyhow they were all playing out, having fun as all kids did in the seventies, Myself? Well having seen them all for the first time I darted into our new garden through the gate posts, I say gate posts and not a gate because in all the time we lived on Keswick Drive mum never once rang the corporation for a new one.

So here I am in my new garden, new surroundings, keen to explore everywhere, and the perfect place to hide from those mad kids over the road. There was Smells of summer in the air, and sounds of distant ice cream vans jingles - Antonio's and Rossi's ice cream men I came to know well their van jingles ringing in my ears daily.

Fox on the Run by The Sweet was in the charts at the time along with seasons in the sun, I used to dial them on our phone at the bottom of the stairs when Mum wasn't watching of course. I ran her bill up once and we had it cut off cos of dial a disc, back to my new home and there was an archway that separated our house from our neighbour Jenny , Jenny was a bit of a rough-looking woman she wore flared denim jeans and jumpers that came halfway up her belly she spoke with a Stockton on tees accent she knew how to live her life though and how to look after herself abundant in street cred not intimidated by anyone at all wasn't Jenny on our street and she did not care what folk thought of her either.

She had many run-ins with the neighbours and if it seems I'm painting her here as a rough one here then yes, she was, but equally, she seriously had a heart of gold too especially towards my mum and would help her out whenever she could she always had mums back. She would drop in every day for a cup of tea and gossip with my mum. Mostly moaning about her husband, Mick who worked at the local dairy on Drury lane opposite old library never being home and when he did all he did she would groan on at mum that he was a slouch and always falling asleep on their settee.

She would also regularly hint she was skint, anxiously waiting for mum to stretch out her helping hand, which mum being mum normally would, even though mum was skint herself she still helped her out. If Jenny's heart was made of gold my mums were platinum.
Anyway, where were we? So Yeah, I just remember running through this archway that separated us from Jenny, it led into our back garden and for the first time in my life I saw, to my amazement, grass! We never had grass in our backyard on Wilson Terrace or come to think of it any house we had lived in. I thought only posh folk had grass like in the stories my Nan used to read us. Seemed to me That removal wagon had dropped me in the pages of a storybook - Nan's stories in my mind suddenly seemed true.

Further reinforced in my little developing mind when I discovered our shed, the outhouse as it was called, on the concrete floor. There was this rather large looking white rock shimmering with what looked like emeralds or rubies all over it. Excitedly I rolled it out the outhouse and called over my mum. " here look at this what I've found mam I think we're going to be rich, I think I've found treasure," And I said this in a real convinced manner "Sell it on market mum we might be rich nah " mum smiled at me patted me on the head with a wry smile and said, "aye Probably love I,I do it next week then , she walked off then almost as an afterthought she says "and while you're at it why don't you go find us some more that should keep you busy all day while I unpack "And so, hanging onto mums word I did as she asked, minutes turned hours, hours turned to days, and the days turned to weeks, still nothing, But I stuck at

it, digging frantically digging and more digging in the hope I would find more buried treasure for me, mam. I was six years old my imagination had no limits I was not yet tainted by Adulthood and in my mind, I would find more of that elusive pirate's treasure it was just a matter of time before I struck gold until a few weeks later the harsh reality began sinking in. Mum would ask me with an almost sarcastic tone of voice "found any more yet love"? "nope not yet mum I don't think there is any more mum" my enthusiasm at this point had wained a little the only thing I found was some old potatoes,and also it was back-breaking work searching for that treasure here picture this I was right short me and skinny as a rake and the spade was bigger than me an all, so I had to jump on it a few times to dig it in the soil properly I sweated like a pig. Anyway we did end up with a well-dug garden though which I think was mums plan all along, sneaky was my mum sometimes she conned me all along it was a con she got a well dug over backyard off back of my sweat while all I wanted to was find treasure she exploited me, however, it was a blessing in disguise as I came to love that garden, mum bought me some carrot seeds once and said "grow these if you're bored love" and I did every morning before breakfast I would run downstairs to see if they had grown , I loved watching the veg sprout through the soil. So, without realising it at the time, I began to grow the family vegetables – lettuce, radish, peas, carrots, potatoes, spring onions, turnips, beetroot -. Boy, I dug that back garden over and over every square inch of it Took me days it did, weeks even, a pure back-breaking effort not bad for a six-year-old kid!
My feet often throbbed an all cos I only had a pair of pumps to wear, it hurt like hell. But my garden was also a great place and a perfect excuse to hide away from
Those annoying kids in the street, one day whilst I was walking proudly between my lettuce patch, those annoying noisy kids playing outside my front garden making a noise. Whenever they did catch a rare glimpse of me when I wandered into the front garden they would approach our gateposts with the usual demands " here what's your name you? do you want to play with us? tell us your name?
I used to think to myself, when they asked me this, go on Jonny tell them if they carry on annoying you tell em "here you lot Come in this garden you lot and I'll report you all to the council" anyway my stubborn resistance wasn't to last and those thoughts did eventually subside and one day with a deep breath and a gutsy attitude I reluctantly gave in to their demands.

Yes, it took me quite a while to reluctantly reach out my hand of friendship to them, not because I was shy or anything but as I mentioned earlier I never had friends until the age of six until I moved to Flanshaw. So, my first Friend on Keswick Drive was a lad named Kevin, can't think for the life in me how we first met but I remember him having a Scalextric set in his front bedroom., we used to play for hours on it, it had red and blue cars, his mum and dad Helen and Tony were great to me too, when I was round there house and the only time she would stop me playing there was when she would shout Kev for his dinner. Other days we would play in his backyard, his dad, Tony, was a keen gardener and they had a beautiful garden, front and back with a lovely lawn, Tony was always watering the grass spraying the flowers etc I'll Never forget the smell of flowers in their garden – cos it was beautiful.

Now let me just say Kev was a good friend of mine, still is. The very first in fact. And as well as being my first friend he also, happened to be my first fight an all, I'm guessing looking back on it, it was all a bit silly one day for no reason at all he just kept asking let's have a fight? it probably was his first fight as it was mine and my last if I remember, I just remember us going on the field taking our jumpers off and having a ding dong I can remember nothing of note, in fact, Kev if anything was getting the better of me until I came up with this absolutely lucky punch, hit him on the end of his nose I did. The blood ran from it like a tap. I was shocked and felt awful cos he was my mate anyhow the fight ended there and then, and Kev walked off whilst I ran alongside him asking "are you ok?" funny thing about childhood fights, we became closer mates afterwards. I still speak to him now and then, and also Andy, his younger Brother, although I don't remember Andrew as well as I did Kev, but recently I met up with him and his young Son Dan who is now a race driver lovely lad driven and very talented, just a lovely family all of them to my sadness they moved off Keswick six years later.

My second friend was a boy called Michael Charlesworth I got to know him because one day his sister, Lisa, and her best friend Susan Heslop, Michelle James and a few others were in their front garden playing in there Wendy house. They lived directly opposite to our house and they were acting out some kind of girly game with a table-cloth on the lawn dolls in plastic chairs. Michael came up to me and asked "Here Can I play with you, Jonny? cos I hate girls me my sister does my head in an all" and he said it in a frustrated sort of voice and an anguished look on his face, I could see his pain and I reluctantly agreed as long as he let me have a ride on his yellow Chopper Bike Five gear deluxe it was. In heaven I was. We spent the whole day taking turns crogging one another. It's all we ever did as far as I can remember really, was ride his Chopper bike. We also enjoyed, jumping across his outhouse shed roof onto Mr's Prince's outhouse other side of Ginnel without her knowing obviously. Janet had a son called Gavin, and Gavin loved his bikes, he rode a Budgie bike whilst his older brother Michael, the quieter one of the two owned a Tomahawk, both of which looked like a Chopper only smaller, the Budgie being the smallest of the two.

Anyway, we would climb his outhouse in the backyard and jump across the gap between Mr's Prince's, it was quite a gap you know, and it really did take nerves of steel to jump across it as there was a good 10ft drop onto the concrete below if you missed. This ginnel also had an arch at the end of it that led onto Wasdale Road and when we weren't hopping the sheds we would be climbing this arch, strategically placing our feet either side of it and shimmying all the way up, easy a good 15 feet, finally sitting on the top of it excitedly celebrating as though we had just climbed Mount Everest. Heart-stopping stuff for our parents, fun for us, boy did we danced the razor's edge as kids in seventies? No Fear either or owt

We didn't see the danger, we only saw the fun of it all and the challenge. We truly lived on the edge, and why? well because we could, our parents had nightmares, we often got a telling off from them about it but it never stopped us. the only thing that could ever stop us, was the regular almost like clockwork Jingle in the air of Antonio's ice cream van.

Chapter Two

Sticklebacks and Catfish

And so, onto my next mate, a giant of a lad called Gordon, AKA Godis. A few months after moving it was now approaching my 7th birthday and I was doing my usual routine, seeing to my back garden veg patch and pottering about in the front garden. Mick over the road wasn't playing out. And I was bored, kicking stones on the pavement just outside my gate posts thinking of something to do. I had been playing hop-scotch in our archway earlier with my brother and sister but Jenny Exley's brother David, a tall muscular bloke nasty man by nature an all, came out shouting at us scared life out of us "trying to sleep in there shut it" he said one time angrily at us. So, we heeded his warning, and this particular day because I had nowt to do my mum bought me a packet of sunflower seeds later that day to try and kill my boredom. I remember planting them in the front garden right under the hedge and as I was doing so I looked over my shoulder and noticed this giant of a lad playing in his garden with some kind of throwing instrument. A kind of stick with a weight on the end and I was fascinated!!!! So, I mustered up my courage and shouted over

"Here what's that you're playing with?". We never used the terms mate or pal in the '70s, they were words that were never heard of, so I shouted: "here What's that thing you're throwing?" Godis shouts back "It's a Bobby Arrow, why?" spoken in a reluctant, 'don't talk to me leave me alone kind of tone.
I felt a bit intimidated at first, to be honest cos he was a big lad Godis, a few years older than me an all and twice the size. Anyway, I remember saying "Throw it in my garden" "No" he replied, "no chance get lost you, fathead if u want a throw then come over here".
Fathead? I thought, what's one of those? a fat head? I thought, Anyway I went over to his garden and walks through his wooden gate.

"I'm Godis what's your name?" he asked. "Oh, I'm Jonny" I replied, in a sort of nervous, shy voice, and with no pause I asked, "Can I have a throw then?", "Yeah if you want," said Godis. So, I did I threw it hoping it would land in my garden, but I never realized the Bobby Arrow was designed to fly to the moon, and Gordon never told me this thing could have landed on the on it if you threw hard enough, Anyway, it landed in a garden next door but three to mine and the man's garden it landed in was a copper called, of all things Bobbie Allan!

He was a scary man, rather big-built with a brown pin-striped suit. Hardly ever smiled much either, and when we went to retrieve it from his garden he came out and said "Oi Out of my garden. Here take it, but if it lands in, here again, you're not having it back got it? Go Play in your own half of street" So, there you have it my first encounter with the streets grump, Bobbie Allan RIP.

So, by end of the week I had made four friends much different from one another, the best of both worlds, Mick with his chopper bike, Gordon with his Bobby Arrow, Kev with his Scalextric set and by now I was Kind of acquainted with Michael and Gavin Prince but yet to make friends with them properly but I did later on . And besides this making friends was not so bad as I thought really and plus they all had great toys, so back to me and Godis not long after that encounter with Bobby Allen, we went to a field at end of the road, the likes of which I had never seen before. A massive playing field it was, still is to this day.

Gordon asked me "Do you want to come to play on Grazzy field?". Confused as to what he meant, I agreed all the same. I ran alongside him, cos Godis was big and his one stride I would have to stride three.

Anyway, we got to the end of the street and there, across the road was this enormous field I recognised it as the place me and Kev had fought weeks previously. We ran across to it and, spent the whole day there, throwing this Bobby Arrow up and down I remember the smell of fresh cut grass in the air and the warm sun beating down on our bare backs we only wore shorts an all it's all we needed. "What's this?" I curiously asked Godis "Oh that," he replied, "that? it's a cricket pitch haven't you ever seen one before?" Well yes, I had only this was concrete, not grass. We ended up playing on that too later on with a cricket bat Godis's dad owned and a corky ball from hell. Which scared the beJesus out of me especially when Godis was Bowling.

So, a whole day spent on what I knew now as Grazzy field and when we got bored playing with his Bobby arrow, Godis walked me over to what looked to me like a river.

He explained that this is was where he goes fishing for sticklebacks and catfish. I had no idea what he meant by that until the following day when he got his fishing net out of his shed from the side of his house. It had all sorts in there, old spanners and tools of all kinds of his dads including his dad Alan's prized tomato plants that he used to grow and various heavy tools. On top of the shed was an old wooden sledge we had fun with that too but that's for later in my Tale.

So anyway, Godis said to me "Jonny go ask your mum to give you twopence for a fishing net". So, I did and we walked up the hill past the tennis courts, in months to come, we would pay this lady who owned it five pence for a racket each and a few tennis balls, anyway, that's another tale So we get to a shop called Slacks. it sold all kinds of stuff for the local kids - from fishing nets to Lucky Bags, pretend tattoos, elastic band wind up aeroplanes kites and of course my favourite sweets at the time, Spangles. I walk into this shop, there was all these adults and kids taking money out. I always thought you spent money in a shop not take it out, but later my mum explained to me, it was also a 'penny bank'. In fact, she opened us all an account there not long after. I saved money up for Christmas presents in that penny bank used to buy my brother in law Richard a cigar every Christmas with my carol singing money and my mum an ornament of some kind for her china cabinet

Anyway, I bought a yellow fishing net with my two pence and we headed over the road to Flanshaw Beck.

I never to this day have ever forgotten the smell it of that beck either. A stale fishy kind of smell mixed in with what I believe was the dyes they used at the mill further up, I remember the smell of the flowers in and around its bank too. Buttercups, daffodils and a tree that hung over its water's edge that late we often made a Tarzan on. it also had these strange-looking weeds, purple in colour, and when you touched them they would explode, Godis said they were called Policeman Helmets. So, we're down by the beck, balancing on these old stones that protruded from the water's surface under the beaten old wooden bridge clear rushing water flowed under it.

Godis and I would take it in turns, we had a clever way of catching the more elusive of the two species we called a catfish much bigger than a stickleback and such a prize if you caught one, he'd lift a stone and I would gently hover my net over the stone waiting for a catfish to swim into my net, we caught loads doing it this way even had a bucket to put them all in and would pour them back in at the end of the day for us to catch for some other time .
So, there you have it long, hot, summer seventies days, that's what it was all about. They were the best times in the world, growing up, I was starting to enjoy life and living in this new home Flanshaw. Well, after this me and Godis, pretty much became good friends too, and soon after my brother Mick was too joined in with our adventures. And in a few years our Mick become Godis's best We were the terrible trio for a good few years and caught loads of fish, and embarked upon many of an adventure which you will find out later but for now, read on. Well catching all these fish, I did not want to pour them back in the Beck so one day my neighbour Jenny gave me an old ceramic sink - god knows where she got it from but I thanked her and we sank it into our back garden and began putting our days catch in there soon filled it too we even filled it with newts from a pond that used to be opposite British Beef on Flanshaw way.

I met many good friends on Keswick Drive over the years. Martin Furness, a tall gangly skinny lad but kind natured had a bit of a temper sometimes when he wanted to, mostly with his sister Melanie if they had been arguing which they did a lot that brother-sister relationship you know? they often wound one another up, they moved on to Keswick as my old friend I never really got to know properly moved out called him Shaun he had a problem with his hip and wore a calliper but a nice lad and a touch reserved with me at the time. And Eventually Michael and Gavin who lived next door to Michael Charlesworth also became my mates as well Michael prince used to let me ride his bike behind the granny flats out the way of his mum Janet in case she saw me she would not have been happy because I used it for jumping over my mates in the garages at the back of the granny flats. I hammered that little old bike

So, the Days and months passed. Every day we would all play in the street, the number one song at the time was Seasons in the Sun, I loved that record this song sparked my interest in music, and. Then not long after, a band came along good-looking Scottish lads from Glasgow called The Bay City Rollers.

Well thanks to them this proved a turning point in my life and as I hit the ripe old age of seven and a bit, I was well and truly into them. Mum bought me a pair of white denim trousers from a jumble sale, and I remember thinking 'Wow, Les McEwan lead singer wears a pair of these'. Only this particular pair didn't have the tartan down each side of the legs. So, I needed some tartan for the finishing touch to look like Lez McEwan a mission ensued, and low and behold while climbing of bales of old clothes as we did regular back then I found some in an old bale-stack at a place called Walkers Mill and spent the whole morning cutting it into strips. I asked my mum for a needle and cotton and began sewing away. By the time I had finished them, they looked rather cool and befitting of a roller like me, a job is well done if I'm honest.

So, there I was, listening to Shang a Lang on the radiogram in our living room under the window. feeling rather cool with my home-made white denim flares in my hands showing off my handy work to my Brother Mick who took no interest whatsoever in my handy tartan work downsides of the legs "Mum," I shouted, "I've finished. Have a look "Go on then love, try them on!". Mum said So, I did a disaster though Being so keen to look like Les McEwan and wrapped up in my enthusiasm to get the job done I not only had sown the tartan to the legs, but I had sewn the legs to the tartan an all, and as much as I tried to save face I simply could not I couldn't get my legs in them.

Mum just sat there laughing at me our Mick had a dig an all, so I did what I always did I threw a tantrum I ran upstairs to my bedroom in shame. I spent the whole morning in their throwing things all over the place until Mum came upstairs and shouted at me "Stop being a big baby, bloody idiot. Giz em here I'll do them for you, you morngy little sod". And There you have it my introduction into the world of pop music, and after mum's great efforts Shang a Lang folks, I finally looked like a Roller. Mums always know best as they say.

Along came our first Christmas on flanshaw. It's hard to put into words the magical time those Christmas's brought me as a kid back in the seventies. On Flanshaw, the television always ran that Milk Tray ad with a James Bond bloke jumping over mountains to give this good-looking bird a box of chocolates.

The films they would run an all that you would never get to see on telly normally it felt like the tv was giving us a real treat for a few weeks movies and tv shows we never ever dreamed of seeing until Christmas came along were now showing on our telly mum used to love buying the tv and radio times too to look through the pages to see what was on she would sit there with a pen marking off what to watch.

Then the hampers got delivered, Mum used to buy from the catalogue an all. I remember the box being filled with these white polystyrene balls and, once you fought your way through them, there would be such delights as Pek Ham, Ritz crackers. Biscuits of all kinds shapes and flavours and instead of throwing away the hamper boxes she gave them to me and my siblings to play with we made dens out of them we had imagination what can I say? She also had booze hamper with sherry and black beer and on Christmas Eve she would mix black beer with lemonade and let us all have a drink.

I would always pretend to be drunk and fall, wobbling around the room. Which made mum laugh, and also me and my siblings would look through mum's catalogue and play a game that she once made up for us back on Thornes. She would say to us "You all have £500.00, you all own your own house I want you to cut out all the things you will need for your new house with the £500.00." What An awesome game I think Mum made it up as a way to keep us all quiet and stop arguing amongst ourselves over who was going to help her put all the hamper food away in the cupboards, but I think deep down it was more to do with her teaching us all to handle money better than she ever did, a life skill for when we got older.

Looking back though it was a bit annoying really, because for one I was crap with money, still am My siblings were not though they were always very clever, and make fun of me because I would end up with just a telly and a sofa and the rest of the money I had left would go on games Ker-plunk, Mouse Trap, Evil Knievel's bike, I loved that oh and the Bionic Man

an all - he was my hero I bought them all who needed a cooker I wouldn't have time to eat if I was playing with my toys so sod I thought ,
Besides These were my childhood heroes, I once remember watching Evil Knievel jump thirteen double-decker buses at Wembley on World of Sport one Saturday morning I'll never forget the sight of him falling off at the end of his jump, he looked like a rag doll and I truly believed I had just witnessed him die in front of my eyes I also felt at the time my childhood was over cos Evel Knievel was to me like the perfect dad I never had. My heart was thumping watching him whenever he performed a jump. A massive influence on me, and I'm guessing 99% of most kids back in the seventies.

So, where were we? Yes, back to this dream catalogue house. Well, it was a sort of seventies version of a man cave really. Minus a cooker of course, or a telly my siblings always did the best with their money they were boring I had my own ideas on pretending to be a grown-up, how to spend money, how my house should look etc and they had theirs

Anyway, cut a long story I failed miserably they ended up with right posh houses and a few toys I ended up with an empty house lots of toys and a sofa.
Also back in the seventies, there were lots of random power cuts too, More or less every night Mum would always have candles ready as she had grown up as a child under candlelight, sometimes thought she would forget not often but she did and she would send me to GK Hall's for supplies. They were packed in a red stripy box and when the lights went out we would all cuddle up on the sofa with a blanket and sit under the shimmering light of our coal fire I vividly remember looking up at our ceiling as its flames shadows seemed to dance on the ceiling we would burn old clothes, an all wood, anything we could get our hands on in the winter on that old coal fire, to keep us warm. To survive Mum even taught us how to make home-made firelighters from an old wakey express newspaper.
Strips of newspaper twisted tightly into a sort of knot and placed between the wood and old clothes, or coal if we were lucky, and Mum would then light the fire, usually with a page from the Wakey express because it was broadsheet back in those days and it fitted the broken glass in front of the fire perfect,

We never had much money, then again, he was not exclusive a lot of families back then didn't, but it's the memories folks, the simple things in life as they say, and when we had nothing to burn Mum was a survivor she would fetch the blankets down from upstairs and we would all jump under those, it was that simple and it was that straightforward we survived any way we could. especially on those dark, snowy, winter nights, either we did the above or we would all go to bed early. We could not afford a portable TV so mum would often struggle and carry our bulky TV upstairs for us and we would watch old Frankenstein and Dracula films and scare ourselves to sleep.

Money was tight of course it was, but every Saturday I always# made a bit Doing errands and bob-a-jobs for folk on our street I earned around £2 every Saturday morning going to fish shop for folk. I tidied gardens picking litter up for Mr's James's mum who lived next door to Cath she always sneaked me a strawberry cream bun an all,
But as a kid and at the time I Never thought for one moment we were struggling , Mum was good at hiding it, but sometimes god knows how I knew but I noticed her quiet and deep in thought and I knew she was skint I knew she was and I know she was missing Nan Because Nan always made it right, anyway I would give her some of mine for what she needed and all she ever wanted from me was money for a loaf of bread or to buy tins of beans or milk never anything for her it was always for us .

So anyway, we would watch the Xmas TV schedule mum had marked up. The weather outside was freezing, the wind was howling and snow came down heavily. I will never forget the smell of pine from our Christmas tree especially in the morning and the smell of coal in the atmosphere spewing from the chimney stacks in the street when I walked to school and at night smoking away under the starry sky and our streets were lit with white lights back then not orange. And Going to school at Christmas I remember making collages out of paste shells stuck on this coloured card with sticky white Marvin glue, then the teacher would get out the glitter for us to sprinkle on it and then we would proudly take our work home and stick it on the front wall over the fireplace.
We made Christmas trees and all sorts to take home. I loved arts and craft at school and our art teacher at St Paul's, I remember, was a bit of a hippy with a hippy long hair cut - I couldn't wait to leave Saint Paul's though

because I hated one of the teachers, my class teacher Mr Nutting. I hated him, he made me nervous cos he would shout a lot especially at me He seemed to pick on me a lot for no reason,

So, Christmas 1974 came and went, also memories of my Auntie Edith and uncle Stanley's Xmas parties we would attend over in Batley. They always threw one every year even threw them for no reason whatsoever, the seventies were like that though, that's what families did back then it was all about friends and family being close ,Aunt Edith and Uncle Stanley would throw parties randomly out of the blue, Uncle Stanley would pull up outside our house in his gold Ford Granada, the seats inside it were comfier than our settee, Auntie Edith loved the parties too as it gave her reason to get the crystal to wear decanters out and the big brandy glasses from the china cabinets. I'll never forget the pineapple and cheese cocktail sticks she used to make either and the mini sausages, egg-filled pork pie and salmon and beef spread sarnies and the massive cat they had called Snowy.

She was as big as a fireside rug I swear, looked like one too no shit either, a big white fluffy thing the likes of which will probably never be seen again, she must have been an experiment in a lab somewhere that went wrong, god knows what they fed it, and my uncle Stanley, an extroverted bloke, he wore a sheepskin coat and a flat cap long before del boy hit our screens. But he had heart of gold and he loved us all like his own. He was awesome, Uncle Stanley,

It wasn't until later in life after losing him I realised how much I learned from him basically if you have an idea go with it and go with it with passion. That was Uncle Stanley That's how he rolled, he was an eccentric and often funny man and Aunt Edith the complete opposite two beautiful human beings who sadly are no longer with me.

So, after the wild Christmas parties and the new year's party mum always shed a tear at midnight when we sang Auld Lang Syne because New Year's Day was the day we lost Nan we all thought of Nan on this day and New year was never about celebrations for me as a kid it was always about Nan even to this day I sit for a few moments in silence to remember her

So along came 1975 The weather outside was still freezing, snow falling off our roof onto the paving flags below our front window

I used to sit at the window perched on our radiogram and watch it it was seriously heavy and the flakes so big and it got so deep it would come right up to our front window ledge.

And At night-time, whilst laid in bed, under my cotton blanket, I remember laying there and even though the lights were off most the time cos of the power cuts, our back bedroom always looked illuminated on the ceiling because of the snow reflection outside under the moonlight.

I was always curious when it snowed whilst laid in bed, I could never settle wondering in my head how deeper it had got every five minutes or so, so I would sneak quietly to the windows as to not wake my sister Edith up and her husband Richard they shared our bedroom with me and our Mick. My brother in law Richard separated our bedroom with anything he could lay his hands on old sideboards and cupboards as I remember. Our Richard was like a dad to me as a kid he took us all over to the fair on Batley road then to the same one when it left for Clarence park also to the seaside he spent a bloody fortune on us all and even though in years to come he and my sister separated they still remain, good friends, and he always has time for me too, he was and still is a great bloke our Richard.

 Anyway, I sneak to the window to see if it was snowing heavier than it had been five minutes ago.

And through the day I would venture outside and I swear to you right nah that you could hear a pin drop because, back then, a car being a rare thing and only the folk doing well owned one. So, when the snow came down the whole world stopped. Buses included

I will never forget the dead silence as I played in our garden with only the occasional bird singing, making snowmen and igloo bricks out of me mams 2kg stork margarine tubs with Godis and my brother Mick It felt eerie, did the silence, apocalyptic almost!

But as all things end the weather did Eventually, ease the birds, began to sing once more. We all went back to school, my mum bought a record player that summer or did she have it given? anyway, it was great. It's hard to explain how massive an impact it was to own a record player Ours *was a box type with a carry handle on its side red in colour and its texture was a fake leather feel. basically, a box with a lid. We also had a record rack, remember encouraging my brother, who was working at the time to fill it, he filled it with all sorts mostly showadywaddy and mud if I remember he would always come home with a new single every pay-day and when he was at work I would sneak in his bedroom and excitedly switch it on with the knob at the side. When you did this, it made a great clunking noise as the power went to the tiny 4-watt speakers at the front music was to have a profound effect on my life growing up as it did most other kids on Flanshaw. I met new friends later through music because back in the seventies, music was the only real form of entertainment, it was a social thing really for youth.*

Shaping our characters, it shaped our tastes, it made us want to go out and learn about the world around us, even at such a young age it politicized some of us! It did me in my teens, to make friends in a seventies world for youth was through music. Seriously that's how we all rolled. I met another friend around this time an all a neat, well-dressed spikey haired kid from around the corner on Wasdale Road

He wore a black nylon shiny jacket with a golden tiger embroidered on the back and red Doc Martin's yellow laces. I met him one day while playing in the street with Michael Charlesworth, and my brother Mick and Godis.

We were playing a game in our street in that summer, called Pegs girls in our street would also come over and we would all play together a Boys vs Girls tournament. Michelle James Sue Heslop Lisa Charlesworth along with me and my siblings a lass called Tracey who lived next door to Godis we would usually make it first to three! Lots of fun and a few damaged male egos afterwards too if I'm honest.

Hot, sunny days, clear blue skies the smell of cut grass in the air as we played in our street. I could smell the aroma of the neighbourhood's Sunday dinners too when we played out because they wafted through the summer air, Antonio's Ice cream van jingles playing in the distance, and the odd motor car passing by too.

There were not many cars in those days, I think our street had about seven in total - there was even a TR7 - also an old Ford Zephyr owned by Godis's dad Alan, a massive beast of a car with Batmobile wings, green in the colour I think? Anyway, back to this new mate I met Tigger, He rode his Racer with drop-down handlebars past our game, one day right through the middle of it in fact, and without saying sorry he pulled his bike around and he just sat staring at us all without actually saying a word or anything. He just sat there grinning away He was a cool-looking character cool as owt, he just stared at us all as though waiting for one of us to ask him what he wanted. Or why he had ruined our game of pegs. Which I eventually did! " Here Who are you"? I asked. "Me? I'm Steve, who are you? and what's this crap you're playing"? he replied. "It's Pegs, want to play," I said. "Nah it looks boring and I'd rather go for a spin on this than play that crap see yeah".

So, I'm thinking 'umm this guy a bit of a smart arse' The thing is, what you've got to understand about Tigger, he was a bit different to us. He wore different clothes, he spoke differently to us, he had a nicer looking bike than us, his hair was short and spiky too unheard of at the time. he was pretty much a one-off.
I didn't, as most did, feel envious of his confidence I just remember thinking, he's got a nerve to come on our street acting all cool and cocksure of himself'. But He had an air of confidence about him, a touch of cockiness without being nasty with it if you get my drift? We became really close friends for many years after that incident.

In the meantime, and quite randomly remember I said I earned money on weekends here is how I did it, you see I used to go for all the other families on Keswick Drive, the James's, her mum next door, Cath Charlesworth and of course Mr Waltham, with his flat cap. He always stood at the garden gate and would shout "Jonny, do you want to earn yourself 50p lad"? I made over two quid in 1975, going to the shop for half the street on a Saturday morning before World of Sport obviously, wrestling or Evil Knievel was on the telly I never missed that.
And occasionally on top of this, I also did bob-a-jobs too
I'd get 20p from my mum and sometimes 50p off Mrs James and Cath, my mum's coffee friend, and Mrs James senior, but to be quite honest I never knew what to do with it all, never was materialistic,
Yep, I was loaded though and I earned this every single weekend.
Saturdays mostly, mum always wanted a bag of coal fetching for our fire. Mrs James, junior and senior, always wanted 20 Senior Services fish and chips and Cath always wanted a bottle of Lucozade and 20 Benson & Hedges. you could buy cigarettes at that time regardless of age. Added to

this, I often did bob-a-job too tidying gardens of litter remember you're a Womble I used to whistle it to me self-whilst I worked.

Anyway, had to get that out the way because I never explained who I went to shop for, did I?

So anyway, back to the elusive Tigger. He rode off and I didn't see him again until a few days after that encounter while playing pegs, and whilst at the local VG shop on Flanshaw getting some bread for me mam

He pulled up outside and asked "Here Fancy coming for a Crog on my bike? I'll take you home if you want? saves you carrying those bags. What's your name again"? he asked. "Jonny," I said, by now my shyness had pretty much disappeared so I thought 'yeah go on why not, he took me home then we then went to his house and I just remember seeing a large, tired-looking, Bedford van, filled to the rafters with clothes and coat hangers, parked on the sloping drive.

Then walking through the door and thinking 'Wow, this is right posh!' There was this man, big bloke he was, he wore glasses and dressed neatly, sat at on the velvet fabric sofa polishing his shoes. This was Tigger's Dad Bill and then there was Tigger's Mum, Dorothy, who was in the kitchen washing pots and pans and she asked Tigger "Who's this young man than Stephen?" Tigger replied, "Just a new mate mum call him Jonny" replied Tigger.

Mrs Simpson was a beautiful lady and Bill, her husband a fantastic bloke, both of them were, they always treat me like their own. She asked me "Would you like a glass of pop, Jonny I replied shyly and under my breath "Yeah please." Tigger turns to me and says "Want to come and listen to my records in my bedroom?" I agreed and we flew up the stairs turned left and......

The next part of my story is what changed my life forever.

So, I walked through his bedroom door, I remember just standing there still as if in a trance.

His walls were covered in posters of David Bowie. He had a bedside lamp, unheard of in our house, and I noticed on one of the posters of Bowie his hair was the same as Tigger's so that's where the weird haircut comes from then Tigger?" I asked. He just laughed back and said he cut it himself, he then asked: "Who's Tigger?" I said "You!", he said, "why?".

"Cos your jacket, it's ace, in it? it has a Tiger on the back I answered.

"Cool OK," he said. And that I believe, was where his nickname came from - yours truly - I'm pretty sure that's how the story went anyway.

So here I was, sat in his room full of David Bowie posters on the walls, trying to convince him that Bay City Rollers were the thing to be into, he just smiled and said: "Listen to this then , if you think that " He had a record player not one of those with a lid, a proper one with stereo speakers - unheard of at the time, and he pulled out of his record rack a single, passed it to me and said: "Put that on then if you want to hear some right music ".

So, I shut my mouth about Bay City Rollers and reluctantly give him his five minutes of fame. The arm came up, the record dropped, it clunked onto the turntable, the arm swung across and landed on the vinyl ".

Tigger turned up the volume and I noticed he had speakers on either side of his window sill. I had never seen speakers before; my record player was mono.

Anyway, there was the sound of static and crackling oozing from the speakers then, Booooooom! opening guitar riff gene genie hit me like a steam train!

It was at this point, His mum, Dorothy, broke the atmosphere though shouting "Stephen turn that bloody noise down NOW! "

Tigger looked at me just smiled, with this no way that was going to happen expression on his face. Tigger was different to us in the fact that he rebelled a bit against his parents, pretty much unheard of in those days. He stood up opened his bedroom door, muttered to his mum "Yeah I will mum, don't worry about it". Shutting his door, he suddenly stood in front of me and began doing this weird-looking dance, the Bowie Freak it was called, basically miming to lyrics.

I thought 'Bloody hell, this is a bit good and this new mate of mine Christ he is weird as bloody hell, even weirder than I originally thought he was.' Oh, aye and confident bugger an all. We spent the rest of the day with him teaching me this Bowie Freak. It was unreal, a new thing was now in my mind and I changed my musical tastes pretty much that day over to David Bowie.

The Bay City Rollers well I put on the shelf, I still listened to them, but Bowie was for me now, and I eventually learned how to Bowie Freak. It took me ages to learn but I eventually got there days turned into weeks after that day, round at Tigger's. We made a really close friendship, a real bond at the expense of my other mates unfortunately but as a kid that was normal flitting from one mate to another, Tigger also had a Skateboard it had green Krypton wheels, called an alley cat the fastest skateboard wheels money could buy at the time. I rode it more than he did, I rode his bike a red Raleigh Grifter more than he did an all he would ask me all time to go to GK Halls for his favourite sweets Flumps even camped out one summer holiday and did 3 weeks in his backyard, and lived on a daily diet of flumps nicked fresh milk off doorsteps and cartons of orange juice if we were lucky we said to ourselves next year we'll do the whole holidays together me our Mick and Tigger,

My fashion-sense had now changed too, I wanted drainpipe trousers. I didn't want pin-striped, side pocket flares with a tartan that was falling off anymore! Tigger got me a pair from his mum, who happened to work on her second-hand stall in Wakefield So yeah, I changed that day - I woke up to be my own person, to do my own thing, to follow something different instead of the mainstream.
I went against the flow, against the popular and I've been the same ever since really, but if I was to put it down to any particular moment in my life, it was that day in Tigger's Bedroom it clinched the deal.
And so, 1975 came and went. despite knowing Tigger and the time round at his in between this, I still spent a lot of time on our street playing pegs, popping wheelies on Michael Charlesworth's Chopper bike along our street to see how many squares we could clear – 'Squares' you ask?
well, our street was made with what you might call prefab concrete slabs which were joined together that made our street, not the usual tarmac. So, they by their very nature they had a joint in them on each section well using our imaginations we would count the squares as we popped wheelies. I got three squares,
I think it was Gavin Prince who held the record of clearing five though. the streets Wheelie king was Gavin. Also, we played a game called Curby which was throwing a football at the Curb-stone while two people, one at either end of the street, would throw the ball and try hit the Curb - one point for doing so two for catching it, first to ten wins! Godis was

our street champion at Curby, he just seemed to have the knack and he stayed champion for as long as I can remember.

Chapter Three

The Wobblies

So along came 1976 and this was the year that boasted the hottest summer in 350 years, not been beaten since either. The first commercial flight of Concorde took place too, I remember watching it take off on our wooden black and white telly in the corner of our room. It was amazing to watch, even as an 8-year-old I was fascinated with planes.

It felt at the time as though the whole world was changing and seeing Concorde I believed we would all be someday living on the moon like those folk on that telly show space 1999.
But School was around the corner now not primary but big school the middle school but before I write about my miserable time at my new school the Cathedral, I, ll take you on a journey through the summer holidays of that year I want to go back a few months, to the beginning of the summer of this year.

As I just mentioned 1976 was the hottest summer we had for 350 years. It's hard to put into words how hot it actually was, the really high eighties every day on average, this lasted what seemed an eternity, right into the autumn when temperatures were still in the high seventies. Our grass turned yellow so did the grass on Flanshaw hill an all "So, what?" you might ask.

Well as a kid it shaped me, did that summer, I think it shaped a lot of the kids on our street. It brought out the adventurer in me, the explorer if you like? cos for the first time ever I left the safe haven of my garden and wandered beyond the confines of Flanshaw. It was simply too hot not to explore.... and my sunflower an all, I remember my sunflower,

I had planted it in my front garden few months previous and how disappointed I was when it had only grown a few inches, but suddenly along came the summer of 1976 and it grew and it grew and it grew, didn't need much water, it just kept on growing to the size of easily nine feet. Now, you have to remember I was only about 4ft odd then. I just remember thinking about the story my nan used to read us in bed back on Thornes, of how Jack had swapped his cow for a handful of magic beans. I really believed it would grow into the clouds and I even thought that if it did, I would climb it and steal gold off the big, bad giant that lived up there for my mum to buy all the things she ever wanted, cos we didn't have much money - just like young Jack in that story.

Hell yes, though that summer of 1976 brought us the hottest year on record it changed us made some of us boys into men. sweltering under that golden sun and eating ice cream with strawberry juice and nuts from Antonio's we often got our ice cream from him cos he always gave us more than we asked for, he was kind as owt was Antonio, my favourite was his screwballs always got a spare few bubbles when I bought one of these - with my shop money - also his ice cream oysters. oyster-shaped wafer biscuit, jam-packed with ice cream. It would ooze out the sides as you took a bite, they were that good.

Antonio once got into a fight with a rival ice cream van, Rossi's, that had poached our street. You have to understand that, unlike today's ice-cream men, these were real natives of Italy, it wasn't a gimmick to be called Antonio's or Rossi's, these were full blood Italians with a temper to match. One summers afternoon as me our Mick and Godis lay in our front garden we heard this shouting and screaming in a different language to ours. At the time it was shocking to hear someone speak another language other than English, so we all got up and ran from our garden only to see these two ice cream men out of there vans and throwing punches at one another, and shouting and screaming. Wow, I had never seen adults fight before, I thought only kids did this kind of stuff, so it was a shock, to say the least. Anyway, we all agreed Antonio had knocked the crap out of Rossi we only came to this conclusion though because he always had given us extra bubblies god knows who won? I didn't really care I just didn't want Antonio to stop coming down our street.

Anyway, back in our garden So Godis says to us while we were sat eating ice cream "Why don't we have a walk to the Wobblies?" My brother Mick and I turned around and asked "Wobblies? What's Wobblies Godis? "He replied "Oh didn't I tell ye? It's a plot of wasteland at the back of Eastmoor by the pit stacks. My mates at school told me about it the other day and I went to have a look after school to have a play on it." He went on to say "its ace It's like grey sand and it has this weird sort of cement on it and when you walk on it feels like you're walking on water, I swear." laughing as he said this.
"Wow, that sounds fun! I said "Where's Eastmoor?", I curiously asked and excitedly asked " Not so much my brother Mick though, he was always the cooler of us two still is to this day, more pessimistic than me in so many ways an all. So anyway, Godis carries on explaining it to me ignoring our Mick's pessimistic view of it all,

"Well it's miles away but if you're up to it, we'll go if you want," Godis said in an excited voice. Next thing I know, I pick myself up off the lawn and ran into our house, into the kitchen "Mum can we go with Godis to walk on some water? It's not far away."
Mum laughed her head off at me and says "Walk on water? I thought only Jesus could do that?" "No mum, I swear, there's a place not right far away from here, honest. Godis told us and it sounds ace!" I never told her it was a place called Eastmoor we were going to though. Anyway, she agreed "Do you want any water or some sandwiches or anything you before you set off? You'll need some "she asked. "nah We won't be long anyway mum". Mum replied curiously "are you sure? it's very hot out there " Oh no Mum, we'll be fine and with those confident, optimistic words, off we went.

So, there we were, me, Godis and our Mick. The temperature that day was easily in the high 90's, as we set off on what was for me our far away adventure away from Flanshaw for the first time ever. Away from the safe haven of my garden, away from the watchful eyes of me mam as often I would catch whilst out playing in street with me mates peeping through the curtains to make sure we were still alive.

So, for the first time, I was Away from the daily routine on Keswick of pegs and popping wheelies, listening to Bowie with my best mate Tigger, no fishing in the Beck, nothing. As good as all that was today we were to do something new and different for a change.

So off we went into the unknown, felt a bit like Dorothy in the Wizard of Oz that day as we walked through the melting sun-soaked streets, up Balne Lane, along our very own yellow-brick road if you like, as we approached the top of Cliff Hill. Sweat running from my brow, I took my shirt off at this point, it was so hot. "this is a long way from home', I just remember thinking to myself "What if we get lost or something?

What if Godis forgets the way home?" See the thing about Godis, he was bigger than us, bigger than anyone else on Flanshaw come to think of it, also a few years older than us and few stones heavier than our Mick and me. I kind of always put my trust in him for this very reason and always felt safe when he was around. So, Along the sun-baked road we walked, one step in front of the other - left right, left right - like a small army marching into battle.

Having to run as Godis's stride being the size he was had virtually one stride to mine and our Mick's three. Antonio's ice-cream van passed us with its familiar jingle ringing out, I remember thinking this was a totally different world to Flanshaw, big buildings towered above me. "What's this place Godis?" I asked. "oh that?" oh that's a prison where they lock up murderers! That shook me a bit. And then I went on "and what's this place Godis?" I asked Oh, its town Johnny, it's where people go shopping." "Oh right" I replied, "I always thought VG was the only shop in the world everyone goes shopping there surely don't they Godis"?, he just turned looked at me grinning and said, "No, world's bigger than just Keswick Drive Jonny." So, the rest of our Journey the conversation carried on mostly me asking silly questions all the time, Our Mick was quiet most of the way. He was, and still is, a thinker though is our Mick, but I read him like a book and he was secretly deep down just as excited as I was, I just showed my emotion a bit more than him, a lot more even!

Well, we reached this old rusty railway line and I remember these massive coal train bunkers that Godis explained were called rockers, they were on a hinge and would rock side to side. they became our playground too. So, on we marched, this time through long grass, the dry, dusty, sun-baked mud blowing on our sweaty brows from the occasional draft of air. I asked Godis to stop "Godis I need to sit down a minute I'm knackered all this walking." He replied in a laughing tone of voice" ha-ha what's up with you, you soft get? Not far to go now, fathead."

So, we got to this bridge, a massive, blue steel monster it was. But From a distance, it looked as though we were going to simply have to walk across it. so, we eventually reach it "Right we'd best keep our heads down here because the farmer will come out with his salt gun if he sees us!" said Godis. Sudden fright and nerves overcame me I felt conned. I wanted to express my disappointment at Godis but he was bigger than me and also there was the River Calder about 3 feet away from us too and as warm as I felt I did not fancy a dip in there.

 Our Mick didn't hold back though and suddenly spoke for probably the fourth time all the journey" Salt gun?"

"What do you mean a salt gun? and what pissing farmer you fat-head?" he asked Godis in a stern voice, a pissed off tone of voice. aye, our Mick was not a lad of many words, but often when needed he would throw them at his chosen victim with an impact, like arrows flying overhead raining down on the enemy.

As for me, all I could mutter to Godis was "What if he shoots us? I'm crapping me Sen now Godis." Godis said "We'll be alright. Stop moaning, the pair of yh. Look we'll climb these ladders first then run like hell when we're all at the top of the bridge, hide behind the pipe that runs along the middle of it." As he finished these words of comfort I looked up and, only being small, it looked easy a thousand feet in the sky, actually it was about 30 feet but I was only short and I was frightened as hell I was.

So, anyway I took my first step on these rusty old ladders, they creaked as I climbed them an all. The sun was blasting down on my sweaty, hot face now and it seemed to be getting warmer or was it stress? I'm not sure. Step by step I carefully and nervously climbed. Then once on top of the bridge I remember looking across to the other side and thinking 'Oh my

God, I don't want to be here at all, so we set off crawling almost sneaking behind the big pipe that ran down the middle of it, my heart racing at the prospect of being shot out of the sky by old Farmer what's his face. Anyway, we made our way to the other side without incident. But to my horror, the ladders at the other end were even longer of a drop than the ones we had just climbed and climbed down was so much harder an all but we survived that one, what next?

Well, not a lot really apart from the rest of the journey our Mick and Godis still having a moan at each other about us not being told the full story about this blue bridge. Me? I just tagged along only thing my mind now was walking on this water. So, there we were like warriors marching into battle fighting through weeds, nettles and thistles getting stung all over the shop we continued on our journey. Suddenly Godis said, "Over there, look"? There is the long grassy clearing, was what looked to be a pond we so we ran over to it excitedly. "Go on then, get on it!" Godis says to us." So, hundreds of miles later I'm here staring down at this weird-looking grey-coloured pond thingy.

I remember sitting down on the dry dusty mud surrounding it feeling exhausted from our journey and thinking how hot the day was. the sun was getting warmer I felt thirsty but no time for drinks me and our Mick asked Godis to test it out; I thought 'Well if he can walk on it and not sink then we will almost certainly be safe'.

And so, he did and, Wow he ran full pelt across it to the other side and back shouting "wheeee wheeee whoooo fun fun fun" Godis shouts top of his Voice and there was a wave that preceded him as though he was walking on a mini wave. Without even thinking anymore, me and our Mick looked at one another and jumped on it also and we had a blast running from island to island. That went under the trees 'Wobblies', I thought 'argh now it makes sense', a wobbly, watery pond! And so, a whole afternoon was spent, on it, that has to go down as one of my best childhood memories ever.. that day on the Wobblies, the day went on forever but by now my legs were feeling tired and I had developed a bit of a sweat rash not including the nettle stings I'd killed with doc leaves earlier, and the thirst and exhaustion seemed to be creeping up on us all too. Suddenly it dawned on me Why didn't I take Mum's advice and bring some water? 'Mums Know Best' as the saying goes.

So, the brightness of the afternoon began to fade the sun came down over the trees and the heat dropped slightly too, I remember sat there watching the sun on the horizon setting - a burning fiery, bright red ball I also remember birds in the air were singing as we all sat on that dusty hard sun-baked, cracked mud floor, brushing the sand from between our toes that we had got from the Wobblies.

Putting our socks on an old cut-down tree to dry, I then asked: "Godis, here you got any water Godis?". "Nope" he replied with a sly grin on his face I knew then the journey home was going to be hell. By the time we hit Flanshaw we were all ready to drop like flies, the day was cooling down our bodies were not. Most of the time walking home was me moaning cos it was too warm "Godis?", "What?" he replied to me. "It's too warm". Then Godis saying "Shut up moaning will yeah"? this conversation seemed to repeat itself every five minutes or so all the way home in fact. until we reached the side of the Beck near the tin houses by the old council hut and just as I was in mid-sentence having another moan, "Godis" from nowhere started running for no apparent reason He darted off in front of our Mick and me and picks up a piece of paper - a green piece of paper, a pound note piece of paper! So, he's jumping about like a jackrabbit, "Yippee, Yippee, Wooohhooo, look what I've found, look what I've found. A quid, a quid!"

Mad was Godis when he went off on one like that. So much for feeling tired eh? Anyway, the day ended on a high note for Godis, and a resentful, jealous one on my part cos he never shared that quid he found, tight sod! So, after watching a bit of telly with a cup of Horlicks, me mam made us I dropped like a fly that night, laid in bed even though it was a warm, muggy night I slept like a baby on top of the bed sheets.

Not annoying our Edith and Richard for a change I fell fast asleep on top of my blanket as I mentioned earlier We never had quilts back in the seventies unless you were posh of course and then you would own a Continental Quilt cos that's where they came from, very posh indeed and very warm too

Anyhow, childhood on Flanshaw you had to be made of metal cos I'll tell you nah us Flanna kids back then, we ran, we walked, we fought, we fished we played, jumped shed roofs we wheelied our chopper bikes, budgie bikes, Grifter bikes, played on our skateboards, slid down Flanshaw hill when the snow fell We picked apples rhubarb peas nicked cakes from Lyons we spooked ourselves in Saint Pauls churchyard, played *holla, hide and seek, pegs, Curby, football on Grazzy, rounders – we were seriously always on the go and never seemed to eat anything unless it was an ice cream off dear old Antonio.*

As for home and our bedroom, we were never in them, a bedroom was where you slept, hardly ever did you see an overweight kid anywhere when I was at school either Yep, those 70's summers without knowing it at the time turned boys into men.

Chapter Four

The Middle School Years

So, the start of life in middle school soon came along

The summer holiday and our fun at the Wobblies it seemed to come and so quickly though.

I remember going to this place on Balne Lane to get clothes, for our new school they called it YPO), basically a service for low-income families to get school uniform. Never forget our annual visits here every autumn, just before the summer holidays ended. We'd sit in a thin corridor, stacked with boxes of all sizes and the smell of new clothes wafting through the air. Mum always seemed in a rush to get in and out of here and looking back I can understand why.

We always got a navy-blue jumper, a choice of either white or blue shirts, black trousers with pleats and we had a choice of plastic shoes or a cheap version of a boot at the time we know as Monkey Boots. It really was a hard choice between the two really, because they were both crap in all honesty. The YPO version of the boots was an imitation but I always chose them over the shoe cos they slightly looked cooler, to be honest. On top of all that we were given an imitation Snorkel Coat, a sort of blue Nylon Longish Coat with fur around the hood, very warm as I remember - even the YPO version was We also were given black and white pumps for PE. I remember feeling strange and embarrassed at the time cos yes, I had friends who came here too but everyone knew you had YPO clothes at school and it was to prove my downfall after my initiation into middle school.

I fell into the catchment area and ended up at the Cathedral Middle School on Thornes Lane, over the road from the park. I remember going there from Saint Paul's school before we broke up for our summer holidays and having a look around the place. We never did this ritual at primary school we were just dumped there by our parents and picked up at 3 pm, so this tour of the new school we had was really scary for me personally as a kid. So, we pulled up at the gates and I remember thinking 'Oh my god, I really don't want to be here.

My first thoughts of the place were that it was enormous and intimidating. I say this because to me personally, it was a massive jump from a little school I'd got to know so well, I really believed as a kid I would be at Saint Paul's forever. Well, my mum failed to mention until the last minute that I would have to change schools as I got older, it was never explained I thought I would stay at Saint Paul's forever. And to my bad luck, I lived on Keswick Drive which so happened, at the time, to fall under the cathedral catchment area god knows why because Saint Micks was closer to this day I truly think my mum filled forms in wrong.

So, there I was August 1976, looking around this enormous, intimidating building. We walked its corridors I remember to this day the smell of bleach and disinfectant and the floor polish, and the floor had like small, short wooden lattes in a kind of zig-zag pattern - very shiny, very polished, very smart indeed. Also seeing boys much older than me running down its corridors, showing off at the fact and aware that there were us new kids on the show, a nervous new kid in me, may I add.

And so, we walked into its classrooms and I just remember thinking 'Oh these classrooms are massive and look at those desks? they have lids and it turned out we all got one to ourselves as well as our own books to take home and back with wallpaper we also got to have our own pens, and we had to buy a geometry set which contained a compass ruler a rubber and a triangle thing called a protractor - never used the bloody thing. I just remember thinking and having a discussion in my head, 'What am I supposed to do with that? can't I just have my crayons, powder paint and my Janet and John book'? Like at Saint Paul's as for these individual desks with a hole for your pens, I ended up with an ink pen, by the way, not recommended when placed in one's pocket bloody thing leaked all over me new School kegs and on the skin of my leg an all took ages to scrub it off and I got done it off teacher and me mam.

I also remember having to go into the assembly hall and as we walked in the first thing I see is this massive stage like as though we were in a theatre or something like the London Palladium, the echo sound as kids ran up and down its corridors and then the headmaster Mr Speak walked onto the stage this man was as evil as they came he walked onto the stage and in a stern voice simply shouted SIT! by now I just wanted to crawl under a stone at sight of him, just no way I was ever going to enjoy this place it felt intimidating from the off first impressions as they say!! so my first day at Cathedral school started that autumn still warm but also windy the autumn leaves falling from the trees and memories of our summer holidays still ringing in my ears, I would catch this school bus from Wellington street just off Flanshaw lane the bus stop was outside a Betting shop that incidentally is still there to this day and also the bus stop. Anyway, cutting a long story short, I hated it every minute of it going to that school, for some reason well the main reason was this YPO uniform,

I was bullied for having it on the bus and I was bullied at the school because of my appearance and also mainly because most kids that went here didn't need YPO clothes what I had to wear, and kids those days as today could be pretty cruel and they were they hammered me,
I guess if you show you're nervous to a dog the dog will bite and this was the case with me I showed I was afraid. My Brother never had a problem there just me! and it proved my downfall I stopped catching the bus and eventually got the cane for Truanting frequently the School Bobby turned up at our house one morning and drove me there after catching me off school took me into Mr Speaks office and I got the Cane an experience that at the time traumatised me cos, ouch it hurt and I really believed I did not deserve it! Mr speak was a Bully in my mind I hated him he used to call his Canes His Colleague's the weirdo every morning in the assembly he would call out any wrongdoer and wack them with six of his best in front of the whole school, Frightening ey? Anyway, so not long after this Nightmare start to middle school life I was then quickly passed over to a smaller school top of flanshaw road Saint Michaels never knew to this day why I didn't go here in the first place, to be honest. But in all honesty, it was such a long time ago my experience at the Cathedral and a few of those Bullies are now close friends of mine. I bumped into them again when I started High School too but with no problems.

So, after my disastrous start to life in Middle School, the summer holiday of 1977 could not come quick enough.

The queen was coming to town the whole country was celebrating her Jubilee her 25th anniversary on the throne. As a kid it was unreal I blindly admired her then cos of the stories we heard as kids of kings and queens. Stories back in Saint Paul's days I suppose. Austin Mitchell announced on the local news that Wakefield was going to get a visit from Her Majesty the Queen. The Corporation, as it was called then, aggressively and thoroughly gave the town centre a good scrub over— the first it had had in years so that was a bonus if you were a shopper.

My Mum suggested we all dress up in our best clothes and wave a flag for the Queen as she arrived, so that's what we did, me, and my Siblings, all dressed in our best clothes mum made us all line up in front of her. One by one she scrubbed our dirty faces with a damp face cloth. She was always ruthlessly doing this growing up and it fricking hurt an all.

So, there we were outside Wakefield Westgate train station Godis never came by the way while passing his house I asked if he was coming, he said she was a moron and a fascist I had absolutely no idea what he meant. But we carried on uptown I was met with the warm summer breeze in the air and the deafening mishmash of the crowds talking excitedly amongst themselves, cheap plastic Union Jack flags in our hands, my mum had bought from Slacks on Batley Road day before. Then Suddenly in view a woman with a pink coat and a white hat and a tall man at her side, and gold - Wow they wore real gold. I remember thinking at the time if only I could have that necklace, my mum would be rich beyond our wildest dreams!

The Queen waved to the crowd and everyone went wild!

Thing is about Wakefield and you need to understand is nowt ever happened exciting here, I repeat nothing exciting ever happened in Wakefield, It was a massive thing back then for most wakey folk though and I grew up believing she was some kind of goddess and not like the rest of us mere mortals.

She was a person that only existed on our telly at Xmas after dinner. The royal family back in the 1970s were a very quiet, reserved bunch - never really mixed with the public. Proper snobs, as they are today, but then it was worse trust me! So anyway, she came and went and she drove off in her black limo up Westgate with the manic, mad crowds running after her for another glimpse. I just remember thinking 'Why was everyone so excited?'. Were we all so battered down morally that we needed to worship this woman covered from top to toe in gold and diamonds? I mean personally, I suppose, I felt a short-term sense of excitement but in all honesty, I just wanted to go home and play with my mates on the street, and have a game of pegs or Curby, So, the seed was planted that day the Queen had rolled into town and had shown her face and done her duty.

Anyway, we all walked home past Hayley's Mill, over Hayley's field and back on our street were, to my surprise, families with wallpaper tables outside their gates with tons, absolutely tons, of food on them! Well, our street party aside cos it was a tad crap anyway here's what Godis meant earlier when he said she was a moron etc.

So I casually popped up to Godis "So What's this band you keep going about Godis?". "Oh, the Sex Pistols you mean Jonny?", "Yes," I replied curiously. "Who are they when they're at home?". "Oh, they're these right scruffy kids from London and they're as mad as owt, they sing about the Queen." I pondered this for a moment and innocently asked "About the Queen? "What are they mad with the Queen for"? I asked Do you mean cos we're all celebrating cos she's been on throne 25 years or summert? We went to see her the other day, she seemed alright bit snobby but that's about it. how come you didn't come with us? she was nice, a bit boring, but nice. She seemed alright Godis – must admit she had tons of gold on her though ".

Godis replied, laughing away at me, "No Johnny you fathead he had a habit of calling me this, and it often annoyed me," you're a right fat-head you sometimes, these kids, the Sex Pistols, they're shouting and screaming about her, calling her a fascist, a Nazi and a moron and saying that England's doomed with her on the throne!" Godis went on .. And The telly has banned them and everything!" Wow! This was shocking to hear as a ten-year-old kid, but I pursued the subject "OK I did say the parade the other week on Westgate was a bit boring, but our Queen she isn't all that bad surely"?. Anyway, Godis starts singing words to their new song

"Nah Godis that sounds crap." Godis answered "they're going to be massive Jonny, they're banned from telly but you can hear em on the radio." and with this he pulled out a small radio from his jacket pocket a sort of silvery looking thing with a metallic silver speaker at the front with loads of small holes in it and he turned a small plastic black dial at side of it. We heard loads of static in the air as he tuned into Radio One and we sat and waited and then they played it. At this point we had already climbed down from the dodgy built wall, luckily and was laid on the grass in the warm summer sun just by the wooden bridge where a few years back we had fished for sticklebacks and catfish as young, innocent boys.

I just remember hearing this unbelievable strongly played a guitar riff and these drums angrily beating away, a singer screaming into the mic and all coming through Godis's Tiny little transistor radio, tinny as hell it sounded but, What the hell? I was in Shock.

I just remember suffering so much shock that I kept talking I was giddy as hell as it played trying to express my feelings of what it meant to me, the way I felt and then our Mick and Godis, more or less together, shouted "Shut up Jonny.........Let's hear it then you Fathead!"

How the hell do I describe this feeling I felt? Being hit by a steam train comes to mind and dragged along to the gates of hell. But seriously To truly understand what I'm trying to explain here you really need to get into the mindset of only ever having heard John Travolta, Bay City Rollers and the softly played guitar sounds of David Bowie, not forgetting the Eurovision contest and our very own brotherhood of man.

So there I was, 10 years old, just sat there in Grazzy Field begging Godis "lets come to your house and listen to it on your record player Godis? Cos, you have the single don't yeah?" and we did, me and our Mick would pretty much from that day on go around to Godis's and play it in his dining room when his mum and dad were out.

Then he bought the album 'Never Mind the Bollocks Here's the Sex Pistols' from a new music shop in town that had opened just outside the market hall, next to a shop that sold sweets, Wakefield's Pop Inn' absolutely massive part of my childhood that shop became and not just me but population of Wakey .

I was by now in double figures as far as age was concerned and was beginning to stray from the confines of Keswick Drive, we would all go uptown on a Saturday afternoon and visit the Pop inn. It was only small but it was jam-packed with this new style music - Punk Rock - and it sold everything or anything to do with Punk Rock. It had a large selection of Day-Glo pin-on badges and sew-on badges too and I also remember, just around the corner a fat bloke that had a market stall with the best ever collection of punk badges in the world! And you could request owt you wanted putting on them an all. Godis once chose Elvis Is Dead ! it shocked me I wouldn't dare wear a badge saying that I was too unsure of myself at this point and besides I may have got a kicking something Godis never had to worry about.

I just remember seeing the fat man's badge stall on Wakey market for the first time and thinking 'Wow look at this. Oh wow!' Our Mick never took to the Sex Pistols in the way that me and Godis did, he instead chose the Boomtown Rats badges and became a massive fan of them.

I remember wearing a pair of jeans with a few rips I had put in them and a scruffy un-ironed tee shirt, I also had safety pins holding the rips together. I felt a bit uneasy, to be honest, expressing myself to the world how much I had changed overnight, whereas our Mick could choose to wear the punk gear or dress pretty normally as he did most the time, being into the Boomtown Rats was a whole different ball game than being into the Sex Pistols.

He did, however, years later have a Mohican hairstyle and once wore a kilt over some PVC trouser; whereas Godis, he wore pretty much anything he could lay his hands on really. I can remember walking uptown and saying "Look at everyone staring Godis.this is embarrassing" and him saying "yeah, it's fun in it Jonny."? He was, in the early days at least, much more expressive and extroverted than our Mick or I was. Godis simply did not care

We were uptown one day and he decided to have his ears pierced. 'Nice one.' I thought. "Go for it Godis!" I said, then the next thing, I see him walking out a jewellers shop side of the market hall entrance by joke shop with eleven studs running down his earlobe, top to bottom they were! Shocking for a ten-year-old kid to see. Another punk at the time, John Walker, Wacker he did the same and he also dyed Godis's and his own hair once into a leopard skin pattern, but this was later, 78-79 I think. Well, there we were, full-fledged punk rockers at the age of 10, doing things differently than most; dressing differently, walking around getting disgusted stares off the older generation and quite a few our own age too! But it was all good you know. Of course, it was embarrassing at first, it felt really awkward walking uptown on a Saturday afternoon with folk staring at us but I once heard a song by x-ray spex I am a poser and I don't care and after listening to this it got easier that song gave me the confidence to believe in myself. It felt good to live outside the box it gave me confidence to break away from the normal the mundane Bowie as much as liked him was massive but he had already had his revolution in the early seventies - it was our turn now, our generation's turn to take the mantle and shake up the world for a while .

Back at home and My mum had made a new friend over the road Cath she used to go over every night for a cal and a cuppa while I sat at home and listened to me punk rock in my bedroom Cath was a larger than life character she always sat in the chair by the fireside, they had tons of brass ornaments as I remember too and she'd always ask me if I showed up in her living room to see my mum if I would go to the shop and buy her a bottle of Lucozade and a pack of cigs, mainly to get rid of me I think. But hey, I never complained, it was worth the 50 pence. Also, I remember the following week, the Saint Paul's carnival was happening, I remember a float rolling down our street and up Flanshaw hill Lee Whitely another young lad at end of our street excitedly chasing it and us lot chasing it along Batley Road by the horse field. Good times Saint Paul's carnivals they brought the community together, everyone and anyone helped make their floats and dressed up in zany and colourful costumes

Also this year a new film came on screens called Star Wars. I remember watching it at the ABC pictures in Wakefield, afterwards, my mum bought me the sabre sword for my 10th birthday and I used to fly into the outhouse in our backyard in the dark where it would glow and fight my imaginary Darth Vader Foe. It was so different to other toys of the time an all it glowed a bright green and made that sound you know which I mean?. I loved toys as a kid and building things out of nowt I once built a full-scale battle scene model in my bedroom I found an old bit of wood I had rescued from our Bonny dragged it into my bedroom and set to with my imagination I made the hills and fields out of paper mache from me mums Wakey Express she normally put away to light our fire . But that day I made it mine, I then bought a big bag of toy soldiers; blue German soldiers and Green British soldiers from the model shop on Dewsbury road next door to the brick quarry. Basically, I made a 2nd World War battle scene - even had a flashing red-light bulb over it to simulate bomb blasts etc - it was way ahead of its time seriously was right proud of that model I built. Cos I remembered Mrs Fee's lessons about the 2nd World War. That's what gave me the idea in the first place It took me months to recreate, I even bought with my Saturday shop money the artificial grass I covered the paper Mache hills and mountains with it.

So, another fantastic summer holiday came and went as I moved into my new school Saint Michael's in September 1977, no need for catching a bus either so hopefully Free of those bullies, everything seemed right starting here and so it turned out too. Always remember my first day, me and my siblings walking what seemed the longest walk ever up Flanshaw Road. Kids everywhere play fighting on the daily march up there. The Autumn Wind was blowing, leaves falling, a crispness was in the air. Much colder than last year's warm autumn but this first walk to my new school felt awkward, even though I had lived on

Chapter Five

Saint Michaels A Fresh Start

Flanshaw for over Three years now,

I suddenly realized the penny dropped I really knew hardly anyone. My world was Keswick Drive and Wasdale where Tigger lived
So, with that in mind My mind began racing, bad thoughts overtook good ones, I felt as though I was walking to my execution and heading into more bullies. Nerves galore, I walked past the York stone high wall surrounding the grounds and turned left into its gates, along a tarmac drive sloping upwards.
I entered the playground and just remember thinking 'This isn't so bad, it's not massive like the dreaded Cathedral was' and, even though I had worried that maybe this would become Cathedral two, something just felt right. I suddenly realized how small my world had actually been, I was about to meet many more new friends here - friends I still have even to this day.

A bell rang out in the playground and an old looking lady was waving her hand back and forth. There was actually two of them, Dinner Ladies as we called them back in the '70s. Mrs Asquiff was one of them, can't remember the other. So, this bell began to ring out, meaning we all lined up in the playground, the teachers in the playground that day were Mr Helm, Mrs Fee, Mr Barraclough and Mr Jones. They were responsible that day for lining us up into our groups and we were then marched into the assembly hall where a Mr Worth, our headmaster, a weird looking fella with grey hair and a bit of a 50's style quiff going on which would fall over his forehead when he got mad!

I walked through the doors for the first time, long corridors greeted me, smells of newly polished floors which every so often led off its main route into a kind of classroom type of thing with bookshelves and arty stuff on the walls. So, there I was, frogmarched to the assembly hall along with all the other new starters.

I remember the smell of school dinner being cooked and as we walked to the entrance of the assembly hall I noticed these giant mahogany cabinets with glass fronts laden with what appeared to be school trophies, giant silver shields and photos of the school rugby football, netball and rounders teams. Something you have to remember about Saint Mick's, though at the time I was there any way it turns out we had a crap football team really, but the rugby team were champions of all schools - we wiped the floor with rugby - no idea why we couldn't produce a good football team though as after school all the kids on Flanshaw would play a game of footy on Grazzy Field with our jumpers as goal posts. Long before the corporation, erected goal posts around 1979 which I will be covering later. FA, was the game we played and we had excellent players too, goalkeeper Ian Barraclough, myself was a quick left winger I do say so myself, Mark Cook, midfielder, Mark Chapman was a midfielder and there was a host of other good players too Tom McCraw although he was better suited to Rugger as he was a big lad.

Anyway, there I was in the main assembly hall, the teachers were sat in their chairs down the right-hand side of it and we were all herded into sections as I remember it. 4th-year kids at the front just in front of the school stage, complete with its blue velvet curtains, and just to the right of this on the floor was the school piano where Mr Helm always sat with his Clarinet, dressed in his woolly cream cardigan and brown C&A action slacks.

All the way back at the rear of the hall sat us, first-year newbies. Long giant windows to the left of me and climbing frames on the walls that reached right up to the ceiling, I remember staring at these and thinking 'Not a chance I will ever climb those!' and those ropes hanging down as well, I wasn't going to climb them either.

As I sat down on the hard wooden newly polished floor, which had small in length wooden lattes joined together in a zig-zag pattern much like at the cathedral, I looked around me and was in awe at the number of kids there were crammed into a tiny assembly hall that was much smaller than the Cathedrals.

Then suddenly onto the stage came Mr Worth, walking with a bit of a hunched back and a habit of re-adjusting his 50's throwback quiff. He stood behind a sort of wooden altar, a bit like you would find in churches, and he began his sermon to the unwashed, announcing to the school "Welcome back school. I hope your holidays were good ones. I'm looking forward to this year" and so on blah blah blah. Yes, he was boring the whole four years I was there gave me the slipper a few times too. He then proceeded to ask the teachers to stand up and give the school any ideas they might have for the day - this turned out to be the daily assembly ritual.

So, after singing 'We plough the fields and scatter" he then he finished off by welcoming all us new starters. You know, us, the ones pushed to the back of the hall away from the more established kids, the cocky ones who had seen and heard this weird ritual all before. He went on to announce where we would all be placed and with which teacher.

My name was called out and I was placed with a young-looking teacher called Mrs Fee, she was a bit of a hippy looking woman, a bit folky in appearance with long curly brown hair and massive eyes my mate, Lindoln Heald, used to take piss out of her by holding his eyes wide open with his fingers) and she also wore long flowery dresses and boots.

Come to think of it, when I look back now, she was obviously a bra-burner but having said this she turned out to be a really nice, helpful and encouraging teacher. I loved her art classes, lots of powdery paint, plasticine and clay moulding, crepe paper Xmas decorations, collages made with pasta shells, Marvin glue and glitter as we did at Saint Paul's. We used to make all sorts in her art classes, in fact, the previous year there was a band in the charts called Steeleye Span and their song 'All around my hat' was re-released around the time of this school term. Take a listen to it, really reminds me of Mrs Fee and my first full year in a middle school, without playing truant, oh yeah and the singer even looked like her too!

So, were we? Oh yes, a new term, new school, new teacher and new YPO clothes. As I mentioned above Mrs Fee was a really nice teacher but could also have a bit of a temper sometimes. When she got mad, usually for us talking in class when we shouldn't have been, her eyes would grow in size, they kind of expanded to the size of golf balls and would become bloodshot with all the blood pressure I expect!

Our classroom was really big, at the end of the corridor and just before the trophy cabinets. It had large ceramic sinks along one wall and these weird looking taps. On the far wall as you walked in you faced what was mostly made up of large metal framed windows and it had a door leading out onto the grass, where we once collected snowflakes for an experiment with the school microscope.

Did you know every snowflake regardless of size always has six sides first thing I ever learnt and remembered at school was that and I remember our first lesson we were all handed new books and told to back them at home with wallpaper or our favourite magazines etc

Our first lesson which was on a subject about the 2nd world war and Mrs Fee went into detail about how our boys fought in the trenches for our country, to protect us from a nasty man called Hitler and so on and so on. We never saw the realities of war such as I found out many years later but that's another story for another time maybe. So, she handed out blank grenades and even brought out of her storeroom a child's gas mask and standard issue gas masks and we all had to put it on. I hated it! It felt all hot and sticky and when it came to my turn to try it on it was a case of on then off very quickly. We had many interactive lessons with Mrs Fee, she made our lessons interesting.

On to the pupils in our class, I remember my first mate at Saint Mick's - a lad called Darrel Spink. He was a tallish, thin lad with wavy hair a great smile and a bit of a looker too the lasses obviously liked him, and he was a school athlete and his sister Gail both were some of the fastest runners at Saint Mick's.

Anyway, me and Daz met as we were paired up one day to do an experiment involving snowflakes as mentioned above. I was a bit reserved with people at first when I started Saint Mick's, mainly because of the bully experience I had at the Cathedral, but I soon grew out of this state of mind as the term went by.

Also with Mrs Fee I experienced my first school trip with her, we went to a place in Halifax, Hebden Bridge, to watch the old water wheel mills and to learn about cotton production, even got to use an old weavers wheel. When we got back the following day we would watch on the big telly on legs a program called how we used to live Mrs Fee had set her lesson out for us all to make our own cotton from lumps of raw wool which involved a lot of twisting and pulling. She was a great teacher and always made her lessons interesting but It's all I can remember really about my time in that class. Oh, and I remember we once did a lesson about the Queen's Jubilee we had celebrated back in the summer holidays before the school term had begun in that summer of 1977 when everyone went crazy, especially our parents who remembered when she was crowned back in 1952. But having discovered the Sex Pistols I knew different.
So that year came and went
In the summer holidays that followed in 1978.

The fun began with us responsibility to have fun it really did simply come down to us kids as it always had we made our own fun, we climbed, we ran, we played in the street, we climbed Walkers Mill factory roof knowing at any time we could get caught by the security guard who patrolled its grounds – we were always seeking adrenalin rush - hiding behind and jumping the stacks of old clothes made into bales. We would jump off walkers mill factory roof landing 20 feet below onto a pile of coal and go home faces black bright , we jumped the Beck, we made Tarzan's, we built dens, went chubbing hunting for wood for our massive bonfire in our backyard where we often found old dirty mattresses, then we would pile them up in front of our shed we made a game we would take a run and jump and land hope and pray we would land on them or we would somersault onto them, we even had competitions - who could jump the longest away from the shed -I've got absolutely no idea how none of us broke limbs doing this. .
We would paddle in the Beck, fish in the Beck, play top trumps, collect Panini Football cards and swap them in the playground then stick them in our football albums! We'd play marbles in Saint Mick's playground on the iron grates embedded into the playground under the dinner hall windows at home We also would build ramps and jump over our mates on bikes as Evil Knievel did on the telly, even putting lollipop sticks in the spokes to make it sound like his Harley Davidson, usually the least popular person I

would place at the end won't mention names
I was young and into all weird dangerous and wonderful things.

Here I once even did a somersault showing off in front of our Mick and
Godis but instead of landing on the mattress I landed on an old iron bed
spring that hid under the ground from the previous year's Bonny, I
screamed out loud the pain was unbearable Godis and our Mick they
wouldn't stop laughing. "Stop laughing. Don't laugh! Don't laugh!" I
repeated over and over at them. I cried real tears as well, my pain? well, it
just made them laugh even more. And Once our bonfire was stacked full -
we would make dens in it – we'd raid other kid's bonfires an all, usually
the ones we hated! we were never bored no time to be, we also played
holla and hide and seek with what seemed at the time the whole estate
joining in, literally twenty plus or more crazy kids split into teams and
battling against each other through the night when the white street lights
turned on.
This game also was an adrenalin rush, especially if you happened to be on
the opposite side to big Godis because often he would come out of the
shadows and chase you up trees growling like a mad demented mental
person as he did so scary as hell he was.

One time a mate, over the road who had moved into Mr's James's mum's
house next door a funny little lad called Kirk Burnett, he did me a few crap
tattoos once anyway he once fell thirty feet from a tree at the back of
granny flats while being chased by big Godis. I just remember everyone
stood around this tree in the granny flats the game had already stopped
and everyone just staring at the tree and me thinking but he's got
nowhere to hide anymore then we watched as Godis began climbing the
tree to get him, grrr growl went Godis next thing we hear was a loud bang
and bone-crunching sound as Kirk came tumbling to the ground-breaking
poor branches luckily not his bones as he fell to earth but he lived. but
yeah, my god we had fun We raided pea fields, rhubarb fields, apple and
pear orchards. We even raided Lyons Bakery for cakes, buns and pies! We
stole orange cartons off doorsteps and milk too, we hedge-hopped played
knock-a-door run.
We camped out in school holidays we called this early morning mooch.
We used our out-house in the backyard for Ouija board sessions and
snogging girls. And with a smile on my face as I write this no names

mentioned here and also carrying on from where I had left off back in 1974 I made our backyard once again a source of food for our family I grew carrots, peas, Brussels sprouts, onions potatoes, radish, lettuce, spring onions. Seriously we may have had bags of fun but we were also poor as well, as were many families back then. Mum by this time was still I believe anyway finding it difficult to cope after losing her mum and my Nan and we all missed her we truly did, she was the leader in our family always made sure we ate, read us bedtime stories -

Society has changed so much today and as the saying goes (less is often more) and I truly believe that an all, cos kids today well they have the latest Nike Airs or Xbox or PlayStation but they hide away from the world and the fresh air and think that's cool but hey don't worry, I'm not one of those who complain about the youth of today. OLD PUNK REMEMBER! I feel sorry for the youth today, seriously though, what kid who may be reading this with his parents wouldn't feel a bit of envy eh? It saddens me when I see the youth of today - hypnotized by their smartphones and games consoles - hidden away in their bedrooms, missing out on all this stuff we did as kids! They're bored, they're Zombielike even, never have conversations anymore or play out or do anything much really! A rant? Yeah sod it yes, it is.

I personally Think What's needed today is another Punk-style revolution like we had back then. Middle age rant over.

So Later this year, was the winter of 1978, probably my first memory of really heavy snowfall since I was six or seven. One thing I do remember vividly is the snow drifts which were unbelievable. I especially remember a weather warning on the TV, saying that blizzards were on the way that evening; I remember how my siblings and I looked out of our bedroom window from that moment onwards. The winter that year oh my that was a Biggy! Snow like you have never seen. Our garden on Keswick Drive, as were all the others, was completely covered; three maybe four feet. deep in the white stuff. Hedgerows on street collapsed under the strain, we walked to school only to be sent home because the pipes had burst. Not like today where you get sent home if there is a bit of snow on the ground, you only got sent home in the seventies if your school pipes burst. Much of the winter of 1978 was spent at home sat in front of our coal fire, and me running my usual errands and earning money going for bags of coal for me mum; carrying it all home in the snowy blizzards, red cheeks wrapped up in my YPO snorkel jacket and a scarf - pulling an old wooden trolley I had made out of old pram wheels off Jenny next door. It was improvising though and I needed to make a buck obviously.

By this time though Cath Charlesworth did not need Lucozade, Mrs James did not need cigs, everyone needed coal and plenty of it - so I made a good bit of money pulling that old trolley along streets of Flanshaw I remember the bitterly cold wind biting on my forehead and the old woolly socks my mum gave me to put on my hands over my socks she would tell me to put old carrier bags to keep my feet dry.

Anyway, I also had fun too it was snowing, right? So once my chores were out the way we all headed up to Flanshaw Hill. Godis had an old wooden sit-on sledge which had wooden lattes and he polished the runners with, I think, candle wax and we pulled it, me, him and our Mick, along our street, past Mick and Lee Whitley's house, then up the Snicket that separated us from Flanshaw Hill. I can remember walking through this Snicket and looking both ways - up the hill and down it - seeing masses of kids screaming, shouting with laughter as they zoomed at speed past us on their sledges. That was the best winter ever was 1978

So back with Tigger and while Godis and our Mick was busy doing their thing with Boomtown Rats and Pistols I was back around me best mate Tiggers and doing of all things writing a song about a so called friend of ours who we thought annoying at the time can't mention names here though but let's just say the song was about him we spent days writing it, we had massive dreams of it becoming a smash hit and id be sat in his bedroom in my ripped jeans old tee-shirt with sex pistols scrawled across it in marker pen and safety pins all over my jeans and Tigger would wear his jeans usually a white Fonz style tee shirt and he wore a pair of Major Domos these were the rival at the time to doc martins and the tale goes they were comfier than docs , whether that's true or not is subject to debate I suppose but there you have it a kind of picture in your mind as to how we dressed, oh and not forgetting his tiger jacket that had now been replaced with a Lee Cooper Denim jacket .. Always remember when I went around to Tigger's his mum and dad Dorothy and Bill always seemed to have a project going on one thing or another I never saw them once sat on their backsides bored.

Dorothy and her daughter Wendy were doing stuff and chatting away in the kitchen Wendy would normally being expressing her annoyance at her brother Tigger for being the wind-up merchant you see for whatever reason Tigger and Wendy always seemed to fall out over silly little things really just basically your typical sibling arguments etc. Well anyway this particular time Tigger's dad Bill had decided to follow the latest DIY fashion of the time and that was wood panelling !! basically this meant replacing your feature wall fireplace wall etc. with a wood panelling. it was held down with 2" by 1" wooden batons.

I remember Bill with a pencil at the back of his ear concentrating hard on the job at hand he was a great DIY enthusiast and was good at it too. tape measures screwdriver he always came prepared had the best tools an all !! he asked me and Tigger once if we would like to help him me being polite said yes Tigger said no so I went with the latter.

Most the time was spent in Tigger's bedroom writing songs playing his Bowie music and my pistols stuff, we talked girls we were now at that age I guess, we talked about school disco at Saint Mick's wot we'd wear Tigger used to practice his Bowie freak ready for the school disco he was meticulous in his approach and would ask me if he missed anything out he paid so much attention to detail he tuned his Bowie freak to perfection. and that's the other thing about punk though what attracted me to it I didn't need any particular skill all you had to do really was jump up and down and bounce around, no skill or brains needed I guess that's another reason why I became one I had lack of the Grey stuff really. I was a scruffy sod too and punk rock and its fashion sense were perfect at hiding that fact.

So that's that you might think our daily routine summed up in a paragraph! well no not quite cos that year something big was about to happen a craze sweeping sunny California USA at the time called Skateboarding I touched on this earlier, basically a wooden board with roller skate type wheels attached to the bottom and Tigger being Tigger asked his mum and dad to buy him one, so week later I went around and it was there leant against his wall in his bedroom. "what this Tigger?" I asked excitedly "it's my new Skateboard Jonny fancy a go"? Tigger was always generous when it came to letting others play with his toys. he was with me anyway he had nice stuff brand new Raleigh Grifter in red and this amazing awesome fast as hell skateboard I got to ride on more than he did. It had a wide board whereas most in those days were thin boards it also had these mega fast wheels in green called Kryptonics and they were scary took ages to get the hang of them they were best wheels at the time, and I remember just outside his house was a block of tarmac about 10 ft. by 10 ft. on the road and we would use this patch of smooth tarmac to practice our wheelies and 360's on . then one day his mum and dad said there's a new skateboard park in town "do you want to go there, Stephen"? his dad asked. The answer came back yes of course. So there we were outside this massive old looking building on Westgate with our 25 pence admission fees I had a right colorful skateboard me it was a thin looking green board had small plastic red wheels it never actually performed as good as it looked though , so anyway we got into this building the place had only just been built for Skateboards and I'll never forget the smell of the new wood and the aroma of sawdust as we paid our entrance fee they had helmets and knee pads of various sizes they were included in the admission fee and it was separated into two sections, one for the absolute beginners and fenced off from the main expert arena the bigger of the two which was at adjacent to it,

Once in there me and Tigger were strapping on our safety helmets and knee pads we then walked onto the main arena and headed for the beginner pen a man let us through this wooden gate I just remember feeling a tad embarrassed not wanting to show off my pretty crap at the time skills and there was a kind of small ramp at the end of the learner pen the whole floor was on a gentle slope, we got some right speed up on there, I remember thinking this is so much better than the streets we Skated on back on Flanshaw,

loads of kids I had never seen before and who incidentally were pretty good it kind of felt a bit intimidating at first, I felt inferior. We had some good times there and we all got pretty good at skateboarding too, Tigger strangely never went again god knows why he just never did even though he had the best Board money could buy, so after that experience me and my old mate Kev Zelos would go instead also a posh lad from the end of our street named
Daz Harnell, this is how I had met him although I had seen him few years before this when I saw Grease at the ABC with him any way we would all

visit the Skatepark regularly usually each weekend, we had a right blast! Christmas morning 1979 me and my old friend Kev Zelos rode catamaran down Flanshaw hill Christmas morning before any of our parents had got out of bed the streets were a deadly silence as we made our way toward Flanshaw Hill and sitting opposite each other my feet resting on his board his on mine we faced one another each holding the other one's hands and we tremmed down Flanshaw Hill never even giving the cars or danger a though one could have pulled out and flattened us there and then any time and with no mercy. But we did not sense danger it never crossed our minds, but that's how Flanshaw kids lived folks we danced the Razor's edge on many occasion. This proved to be the last time I would see Kev and his Family as they moved from Keswick drive not long after to Norfolk.

Meanwhile back at School it was the perfect place for expressing myself to authority scrawling on my tatty rucksack punk rules OK I bought badges and even eventually bought an Elvis is Dead badge and pinned it along with all my others to my rucksack my school books I had backed with smash hits mags had the anarchy symbol scrawled all over the inside of most of them the lessons I hated the most was geography science metalwork and woodwork hated those, no idea how to measure anything had no interest in ordnance survey maps where Africa was in the world hated making ashtrays and no idea how to make a door hinge either .. simply not interested. The teachers were great, the lessons were not I'm afraid.

So, school was a fantastic time! loads of memories I made a lot of good friends at Saint Mick's Mark Cook Mark Chapman Shane Story Lindon Heald Mark Hibbert John Routledge Timothy Firth Tigger Of course but there were also friends I had started hanging about with out of school too. John Walker (Wack) Tony Everett (Everett) all these went to Saint Mick's but Wack and Everett were a few years older than me though and at the time I only seemed to knock about with them sometimes after school

So, Mark Chapman was a football player very good one too. most of my mates back then none of them were ever into the punk rock scene, to be honest. but strangely we still all seemed to click. Then along came to the football card swap craze, everyone went Panini football card crazy.

I got mine free as I was a paper lad at the time for GK HALL newsagents Geoff the owner used to pay me in cards if I asked politely sometimes. So, what was so special about these cards you might ask? Well, I don't know really. to me personally it just became an addiction each page had your favourite football team and you had to fill in the empty spaces with the players faces I particularly enjoyed collecting the club badge as this usually was a shiny gold or silver !!and every team had its stats page ground attendance etc. times won the championship domestic cups etc.

The arguments we had in the playground over who was the best team who had won what were aplenty, mine was Leeds Utd and so it began I spent ages collecting my footy cards I used to sit in the classroom waiting for the bell to ring so I could run into the playground with Chappy and Cookie. Those two loved their football Chappy was a Man Utd fan and Cookie was a Liverpool fan we used to call him Dalglish cos he looked a bit like Kenny Dalglish always had these rosy red cheeks for some reason! and I sometimes used to squeeze em an all playfully of course which always wound him up.
And we would spend hours doing swaps I once swapped five of my cards mostly Crappy Man Utd players Sammy McElroy one of them Brian Greenhoff another he had been transferred to Man Utd the season previous anyhow I swapped them for the beloved and much sort after Leeds Utd Badge off Chappy, the excitement I got from filling this Footy album was immense and seriously the addiction was crazy and would beat any computer game hands down today!
and when I wasn't filling it with my new additions I was reading the bugger because it was educational too. yeah, so as good as that had been that craze came and went because things moved fast in those days it was one craze after another really. Marbles lobbing a corky ball my mate Kev Lund was school champion at this. Also, rounders dancing in playground hedge hopping knock and run holla hide and seek I could go on and again, here couldn't I? I also remember Shane Storie he owned an Acorn Atom it played tennis two bats a square ball on a green monitor that's it. Computers were few and far between back then and no one seemed interested at the time.

So anyway along came Saint Michael's weekly school disco arranged and organized by Mr. Jones And Mr.'s Fee we would toddle off home on a Tuesday and Thursday after School have our tea play out for a bit tear off our crappy School Uniform then I wore my torn jeans safety pins hanging from them etc. a scruffy old tee shirt only this time I went a bit far in eyes of Mr.'s Fee Cos I naively painted a black Swastika inside a round white circle on a red tee shirt Tigger's Mum had given me I used one of my mums dinner plates to draw the circle as I was useless with a compass ,so I get to the entrance by the reception doors climbed up a few steps and Mr.'s Fee took one look at me and grabbed me by the shoulder her eyes popping out and screaming manically and uncontrollably at me ! she then frog-marched me down the stairs screaming and waving her hands like a bloody psycho and said: "right John either go home NOW and change that tee shirt or you don't come in"! I had no idea why she was being such an ass to me but I never questioned her instead me being me and being the rebel, I chose not to go back that night sod her I thought and walked off saying I, I go home then Miss I don't even know what I've done wrong?

Anyhow when I eventually did turn up the following week and after a lecture on the Monday morning from her about the Nazis I turned up minus the swastika tee shirt I paid at the door Mr.'s Fee greeted me and said "that's better Young Man I then turned to her with my party trick I had planned and smiled a massive cheesy grin at her I had decided to dye my teeth green with food colouring, nothing she could do about that either now was there? No law against smiling was there? also, my hair was red too just to rub it in. It was crap disco if you were a Punk anyway and Mr Jones only played come on everybody by Sid Vicious occasionally he despised the Sex Pistols as did all most the teachers apart from Mr Ferguson. but yes indeed, Food Coloring the perfect cheap accessory if you happened to be a working-class punk, I bought tons of the stuff from VG store on Flanshaw they ran out I bought that much not just me either but our Mick Wack and Godis too we emptied that shop regularly so what if the Sex Pistols were dead in the short time they played together they changed a whole generation of kids! and still had an impact even on today's youth an all.

Lindon Heald and Brian Talbot always got the most airplay of their music tastes ELO Mr Blue Sky and all the Eddie Cochran hits they used to Bop to them all night as punks me and me mates we never got a look in, we spent most our night sat on the school benches that were placed around the perimeter of the assembly hall we would sit there looking all angry and rebellious giving Mr Jones and Mr.'s Fee the stare! Lindoln my mate the ELO fan he was funny though he used to imitate Kenny Everett Sid Snot to me all time always had me in stitches he also once mentioned to me about his first day at Saint Michael's and here's what he told me in his own words

"Wack John Walker!! threw me down the banking the sod!

Wack after doing so apparently had felt bad about it and regretted his actions and asked Lindon if he was ok? Lindoln Replied, "Yeah" no damage was done mate I guess you were just testing aerodynamic theory said

Lindon back at Wacker ...

And also, the time when Fitzy Ian Fitzpatrick broke his legs that winter And the snowball thing I do remember the snow was banging it down, him and cock of school Bolly and John Walker and a few other older ones were making a snowball on the rugby field and somehow it managed to roll down the banking and take poor Fitzy with it, it smashed through the concrete wall and broke his legs.

The drama of it all as we stood there to watch an ambulance driving up the driveway and hear the sirens roaring away

Also, this other memory I was reminded of by Lindon too again (his own words) and I quote

"Mr Smith was trying to hit a six-playing cricket one day showing off and he twatted the corky ball out the school grounds went straight through a bedroom window in acute terrace it damaged we all stood their jaws dropped his ego was damaged beyond repair though cos he had to walk around and apologize to the occupants in front of us all.

Lindoln was also once talking to me about Mr Elm the Psycho Nut teacher from hell who could not play the clarinet too well he remembers him saying this a lot in class when he was pissed off and I too remember it and I quote

"Keep it up buster and you will be on a fizzer" and let's not forget Mr Helms bloopers in the assembly on his Clarinet or his popular Incoming blackboard rubber party trick either.

So, fashion? mine obviously was Punk Lindon Heald used to wear I'm not quite sure now, to be honest, normal clothes maybe I'd say And Mark

Chapter Six

That Winter Of 1978

Cook Mark Chapman Shane Storie always wore normal clothes too they weren't into heavy punk heavy metal or anything Shane was getting a bit into his weird kit at home his prized home computer the Acorn Atom Mark and Cooky loved their football I did too but only collecting the cards. I once played on meadow lane fields one weekend with them in my punk gear a game of five a side with our jumper's goalposts! this is when I realized how bloody fit they were and how unhealthy I was and cos I had curiously experimented with cigarettes s at this point the harsh reality of it all sunk in,

I used to buy separates off Flanshaw swapped empty bottles of Crystivite pop for a single Cig usually a No.10 and a match but that aside for now Let's go back to the Winter of 1978

Snow like you would never imagine! for weeks it came down one of the first memories was looking out my mum's window onto Keswick Drive and I would sit there for hours in our window just watching the snow fall it was so deep it was a struggle for the few cars we had on the street to even open their doors! and so as a 4 ft. nothing scrawny little kid walking out my door after getting home from school and eating me mums favourite fried Onions with mash potatoes bubble and squeak for my tea Whilst watching an episode of crackerjack I would then climb out of my school uniform put on me monkey boots layers and layers of tee shirts few jumpers until I literally looked resembled the Michelin man.

Then mum would give me and our Mick old pairs of woolly socks to put on our hands and a well-used headgear at the time what bank robbers made famous years later a balaclava it was too tight though me mam got the wrong size my face looked all contorted when I looked in mirror at me Sen but I wore it just to please her! so there we were stepping out of our front door couldn't see the few steps cos of all snow that had fallen off our roof so we walked out down the path and knocked on Godis's Door. "is your Gordon playing out"?

I would ask his mum and dad Godis was already, ready though, as though he knew we were calling for him. and he brought his sledge out that had been sat on his Dads Shed roof it was rusty as hell. That is until His Dad and he got the magic candle wax out and wire wool they polished the runners etc. while I and our Mick waited on patiently clapping our hands together to stay warm as all we wanted to do now was to get on Flanshaw Hill.

I can still remember the sounds of kids screaming and shouting having fun the same sound you would hear in the playground etc. And the closer we got to the hill past Mick and Lee Whitley's house. We then walked steadily up and through the little Ginell then bam it hit me

I just remember how bright it all looked the sky I mean cos the street lights back then were white and not orange, on top of this the snow clouds were a greyish white and the two just seemed to come together I a kaleidoscope of colour Which in turn made night time look pretty much like a day! and the cold!! Wow, the cold bit so hard on your face and hands so no time to stand about, Seriously the only way to stay warm was to move and move a lot! never forget us making a ramp out of snow right on top of the short Ginell that separated Flanshaw hill from our estate it led you onto Mick and Lee Whitley's street.

Also, the streets were desolate an almost apocalyptic eerie silence also no public transport or cars they simply could not operate, just a mass of kids from Flanshaw peacock Darnley and other places unknown to me at the time council kids all coming together to have fun in the snow.

Even remember someone bringing a pair of Skis an all! Anyway, me a lad called Biffy John Ogdon Russel Batty Jeff Hudson well we decided to improvise the resources at disposal so we ran over to the Tin houses which at that time were being modernized so piles and piles of stacked corrugated tin lay on the ground we took it upon ourselves to grab a few! they were easy 12 ft. by 4ft in size and made brilliant Sledges, I just remember pulling them up the hill and everyone staring lol then once at the top jumping on it literally 10 maybe 15 kids piled on it as we zoomed at speed down the hill shouting to everyone to get out the way get out the way!!!

Some of my best times were spent on that Flanshaw hill which you shall discover later on in the meantime read on.

So, the snow came and went, but it didn't stop us having fun instead of the snow we would all pitch our brains together and think of alternatives. so, we decided when the weather was a minus in temperature we would pour water on the pavement running alongside the grass on Flanna hill and make ice slides! we would then run and slide along this we used to bend down on our knees and we called that party trick the Diddy Man! And we did all this with no protective head gear or knee pads etc. but hey we survived tough as old boots us flanshaw kids.

"So, there you have it that magical time on Flanshaw hill so we'll move onto 1979 now the end of the decade edging closer and lots of things happening in the big wide world including that woman Thatcher! this was the early beginnings and the start of my politicization aged just 12 It also turned out to my final term at Saint Michael's I had made so many memories here and my life was about to take a turn. Soon to be into my teens wow soon be in double figures thirteen so where do I start?

well for a start I still went around to Godis's for our daily burn out and pogo sessions in his dining room POGO IN like mad demented kids to the Sex Pistols Never Mind the Bollocks Album when his mum and dad went out! never forget once I and our Mick were sat sifting through his record collection while bodies were playing on his record player! then suddenly out of the corner of my eye I see Godis jumping up and down ripped off his tee shirt and was cutting his bare chest with his penknife never known to this day why though? this was crazy stuff. But I suppose it reflected our anger at the system also by now the music was crap in charts, it fell back into this love me the baby type of music again the whole music scene went stale as hell. and maybe Godis was expressing his anger at this! God only knows? well, I certainly felt cheated as Johnny Rotten had said so famously on stage once and as a kid, I was still listening to my beloved Sex Pistols but it was watered down i.e. C'mon everybody silly thing Belson was a gas it all was becoming a bit innocent!! something had to change again and it did the pistols came and went in a flash and music changed quite a lot this year mainly due to the fact a new decade was fast approaching!

So, let's see what changed music forever? well in my opinion Gary Numan He had a song in charts called Cars it was so different I suppose and quite original for the time but not really my cup of tea He didn't have a movement around him or owt a following us kids could all get heavily into none of us owned a black boiler suit either I looked for one I tried I really did.

So, what was this massive thing for me that would take my mind of my heroes the Sex Pistols and Punk rock?

Well I had a mate at the time Mark Hibbert AKA HOBBIT he Bought a madness album a new band at the time and the album was called One Step Beyond I Listened to it in his bedroom one night after school we learned the moves together Chas smash was the dog's nads I swear cool as they come to old Chas Smash.

Not sure how I met Hobbit! I think it was one day in Saint Mick's playground I saw this stockily built lad walking up the drive to school I stopped him just outside dining hall and asked him! "Hey what's that weird looking coat you're wearing? " he turns to me and said, "mate it's a Merton Parker and its what madness wear didn't you see them on top of the pops last night"? I said no, he then opened his sandy coloured rucksack and pulled out this strange looking hat! "wots that when it's at home"? I asked curiously, "oh this is a trilby mate it's what Madness wear you should watch them next week on top of the pops mate " So I wandered off thoughtful in my manner thinking in my head maybe this is what I need? maybe this can replace my sadness at losing the Sex Pistols and Sid Vicious. it would fill a massive void if it could? so, Thursday evening came the following week top of the pops came on and I remember sitting there still dressed in my scruffy jeans and my homemade punk tee shirt and there came on telly MADNESS came on stage I just remember thinking who the hell is that Nutter dancing like a lunatic! it turns out his name was Chas Smash apparently a former madness roadie who followed them everywhere in early days and who the band eventually gave a dancing part to.

well, there was a lot of good music coming through in 1979 XTC Ramones Blondie to name but a few and I was getting into all of it! I just seem to go with what was popular at the time as most kids did really. It was a good time to be a kid was 1979 we were on the verge of a new decade a new prime minister Britain's first female prime minister came to power who nobody had ever heard of and in the coming years most of us wish we hadn't besides she looked like a strict headmistress to me, not a prime minister.

I was as was most of us in our year on the eve of becoming a fully-fledged teenager! this year was packed with things it felt at the time as though we had to squeeze every bit of childhood left out of us, to get it all out of our systems if you like, before we moved on to high school the following year. I spent ages ripping all the fur off my newly acquired canvas green Parker coat my mum got off the seggy market in town so it would look like a Merton Parker.

The Fat man on the market was still around too so I would spend Saturdays up town browsing for badges but this time around not so much the pin on punk badges but the sow on type I remember buying a huge madness badge least 12" by 10" cost me a small fortune and I sowed it on the back of my homemade Merton Parker along with signal red blue and white signal badges eventually sharing my allegiances with the Specials and the rude boy gang even had a go at making my own black and white chequered Tie but that failed miserably so Instead I bought the famous two-tone gangster badge black and white Chequered and cool , even tried to paint it on my Parker but made a mess so covered it with badges .

And the school playtimes me John Routledge Mark Hibbert and quite a few others would get together and do our stomping as it was called then in the playground with a battery powered Ghetto blaster John Fetched into school. dancing to madness mostly, one thing I can say about school it never really taught me much but punk and the music scene did cos it taught me one of the Life's most valuable lessons. That being Confidence and the gift of self-expression without caring what others thought of me, I as many of my pals back then thought outside the box.

And this was down to my early influences of Bowie and the Sex Pistols those walks into town in our punk clothes people sneering and laughing at us it made me stronger as a person even to this day I'm still the same don't care what people think of me I'm Marmite me same with the stomping around in Saint Mick's school playground all these things that at the time looked completely innocent and fun that often got up a few peoples noses actually were the biggest Life's lessons for me , didn't matter to me if I left school my boots filled with pieces of paper to say I had done well and was brainy at remembering what I had been told.

Cos, it never really counted for much back then anyway this education thing. Thatcher had your number and she would keep most of us working class kids in our places in factories mills etc. anyway so what was the point I felt. Obviously, its Different Today Education is so needed for the youth of today many more opportunities and Goals to aim for.

So, 1979 school year was pretty much the most enlightening year of my life at school we crammed so much into it and music really dominated me as it did all my friends we had this togetherness a bond so strong it could never be broken, but it wasn't just friends at school who was into music I would knock about with I hung about with all kinds of characters.

Along streaky looking guy blonde hair the same as mine always wore a scruffy navy-blue school jumper and unironed white shirt like me even had the same hair colour and style as me too. John Ogden his name and what a character he was. Old Oggy think he was first one to get me into smoking actually he and his mate Tom Cotton well they knocked about together a lot and they used to sneak under Mr Helms portacabin classroom and smoke under there cos one day I was trudging back to my class having lost at marbles (again) to Shaun Auty. And I noticed in corner of my eye smoke billowing from under the classroom so I knelt down and there's this lanky skinny lad scruffy looking and a big lad short brown curly hair and he looked hard as nails and he said: "here don't tell anyone youngen will yeah"? well as they were in there last year and I was in the 3rd year I guess they had the bragging rights to call me youngen.

Anyway, he says "don't tell anyone and you can have one if you want"? so I says like an idiot and already had flirted with smoke or two agreed "yeah all right then" so I crawled on my belly under there with them and we smoked like chimneys I just remember feeling dizzy and sick as hell and them two laughing at me. Because those Cigs God knows what they were but they were stronger than ones I had smoked, but yeah after that brief introduction I joined em most days after that for a crafty one, Tom cotton to me was cock of the school but he never pushed his weight about as Bolly did. and I still think he was to this day ...Always looked out for me did Tom.

So, Oggy knew a friend called John Routledge he was a chirpy lad always talking about lasses he had snogged his stories were sometimes interesting but mostly made up. He got into tattoos and as I mentioned earlier in the story he had a tattoo kit in his rucksack Indian ink cotton wool sowing needles box of matches and a penknife looking back I guess 1979 was the year I began to evolve from kid to teenager doing the teenage stuff all the things I mentioned above and other stuff when I *think about it, it was the things that I had experienced that changed my direction and had turned my head if you like.? Over the years I had met morphed from a roller to a Bowie freak to a young punk to a ska mod, nutty boy who still enjoyed a game of marbles and swapping football cards, I was by now turning into a young teenager becoming aware of the world around me and it's in this year that I guess I made that change So, Routledge says to me one day in playground "want a tattoo doing mate"? I said, "how do you mean"? he says "a tattoo! here look at mine" and he rolled up his navy-blue school jumper to reveal a sort of scroll with his name on it! wow,*

I thought a tattoo my hero evil Knievel has some of those so I said with no hesitation "yeah John go on then" we went around the back of Mr Whelan's class and he asked me what I wanted. "don't know just do my name and a cross or something" I said so he did and yes it hurt like bloody hell it was brutal the needle piercing my skin it burnt like hell and all he could do was laugh as he did it.

So, there I was I felt right adult now my first tattoo! oh yes!! and for years I kept it hidden from my mum an all god knows how! I had a few more tattoos after that a spider's web a David Bowie Ziggy Stardust on my forearm all crap still has them an all

So July 1979 we had our sport day and gala and then to finish off the school term Mr. Ferguson our resident punk rocker teacher had, had a word with Mr. Whelan Mr.'s Fee about the possibility us performing an end of school disco they got all us dancers together myself Tigger my brother Mick Tigger's girlfriend at the time Deborah Cromwell among many others and asked us all if we would like to perform our favourite bands singers etc. in front of the whole school there were other participants in this too but can't remember their names now. But anyway, we agreed and would rehearse our songs and moves religiously every dinnertime for the next three weeks or so even practised in Tigger's bedroom him doing the Bowie freak Jean genie, me jumping up and down like a madman to come on everybody by Sid our Mick doing his Boomtown Rats Rat Trap Piece. I wasn't allowed to dance to god save the queen because the school wouldn't allow it Mr Ferguson wanted me to but obviously was over ruled in staff room no doubt, so anyway it was fun having the whole stage to ourselves and practicing it was to be a kind of history of music throughout the years from the Beatles to Kate Bush from Bowie to Boomtown rats to the sex pistols, so the day arrived the final day of the school year all the kids came to school in their own clothes that day as it was non-uniform day and there weren't any lessons either as I can remember I just remember feeling really nervous at thought of getting up on stage in front of over four hundred kids, we spent most the day in the assembly hall and in the morning Mr. Worth announced to the school about our Play all eyes looked at me and our mick smiling some laughing some encouraging I just remember sitting there while Mr Worth called out our names who would be in the play, so anyway way we sang a few hymns listened to teacher announcements watched Mr Whelan nearly fall off his chair again as he fell asleep he did this so often we never even gave it much notice anymore .. and then Mr Helm always finished the assembly off with an Acker Bilk classic stranger on the shore, he still managed to mess it up with his usual loud squeak from his bloody clarinet the school assembly would always laugh out loud and he always took it on the chin though he would stop and apologize to us all in a sarcastic tone of voice that just made the situation more amusing.

So now we fast forward the end of the day approached and the beginning of our end of term play began I just remember the smell of the old curtains and props from various plays over the years at the back of the stage dust all over I had never seen the back of the stage before and it was a weird feeling sat there seeing us all getting prepared and psyched up in our lastminute preparations then suddenly we heard the school hall filling with kids a kind of mumbling sound was heard by all as they all began to talk amongst themselves whilst settling down, it was the sort of noise you would hear in any assembly before the headmaster shouts "silence School" so there we were the youth of the day dressed in our fashions and then the curtain raised I walked out in front of the whole school the stage red green and blue lights fixed on me, the heat from them making began to make me sweat uncontrollably, though a mix of nerves and adrenalin helped me along then suddenly boom Sid comes over loudspeakers it felt weird to be performing a pogo in front of teachers I albeit held in high regard until this point as half on them had never seen me pogo like a looney, and all the school too who most had never heard the sex pistols before or simply did not want to.

but this was my moment, my legs wouldn't move they froze they felt like lead weights and had gone to jelly then the chorus had kicked I had to make my move I was looking a tad silly by now so I took a deep breath and mustered all my courage all the confidence from my early years as a punk came to the fore and I was away, jumping around like a madman I thought to hell with it I don't care anymore what people might think of me after this knowing full well I still had a year left and then it was over I had done it and for a few minutes of my life I felt I had shaken up the world .

Then at the end of my performance the hall fell silent and what seemed like forever it still stayed silent then slowly and very slowly the crowd began to applauded I bowed out I felt like a star a celebrity ha-ha well at least it felt that way anyway.

As it did for Tigger he did an awesome Gene Genie our Mick did a fantastic Bob Geldof Rat Trap A lad called Wayne Batty was on the air drums that day in the background too and Deborah she did a haunting Kate Bush Wuthering height and the sad part of it all was it was to be my brother

Mick Deborah Cromwell and me Best Pal Tigger's last year at Saint Mick's

Chapter Seven

Summer Camp at Tiggers

before they moved on to high school but wow did we all go out with a bang that day I tell yeah that for nowt.

So, the School leaving concert over and done, Tigger one day reminds me of the summer holiday from last year where we slept in his backyard in a tent for a few weeks. This was to be the year we were to do the whole holidays me our Mick and Tigger, so we approached his dad Bill and

Tigger Asked him if we could have a new tent for the occasion we drove off to Mitchell's Camping Centre Near Horbury to choose a tent got it home an hour later it was a four-man tent, and we all laughed in back of His dad's car cos Tigger's dad mentioned it on the way over he says "well boys this should last you the holidays its nylon it's a Four man tent it has plenty of room and has a Bell End for your food. And he said all this so casually as you like. The world stopped before my eyes. We really could not hold ourselves together Tigger's Dad had no idea we were laughing and carried on about how good it was a what a decent purchase it had been but he kept mentioning this Bell End, we all sat in back of his car trying to hide our laughter under our breaths our bellies rapidly at this point had turned into six packs laughing so much but he kept saying it over and over, he knew what he was saying. Bill was a really funny bloke his humour was dry as owt. it got a right laugh out of us anyway. So, once we got home we all went into his backyard by now Tigger for some unknown reason his mood had changed he was arguing with his dad about how best to put it up, it was actually funny hearing father and son going at it in the spirit of cooperation.

so, there we had it a four-man nylon tent with a Bell End for food what more could we possibly need?

So, in the end, and after much debate and tantrums by Tigger it was all set up I flew off home and told my mum what we were doing and she was fine with it I think she just thought wow six weeks kid free! I can go for that so there we were red hot summers day Blue skies above birds singing in the sweet-smelling fresh warm air laid in Tigger's backyard talking amongst ourselves about our adventure we were about to embark upon! Tigger's Mum Dorothy Sorted out some food from her cupboards that she thought would come in handy beans spaghetti hot dog's burgers in gravy crisps etc.

It was awesome She was beautiful Lady Dorothy a heart of gold she gave us an absolute ton of food to last us ages .and we had an awesome time loading it up in that Bell End too! but for all the stockpile of food she gave us it wasn't enough for Tigger he wanted more we were laid in his backyard staring up at the clear blue sky chewing blades of grass and he had a pocket full of money and asked me "here Jonny fancy going to Shop on my Bike and getting us loads of Flumps"? Flumps were a soft marsh mellow kind of sweet and were very popular back then Tigger loved them.

I asked, "how many Tigger "? he thought for a moment took another blade of grass started chewing it turned his head to me and said "ermm let's see", gave it another thought for a few moments and then he said it, he spat out the blade of grass and calmly said in a as you like manner cool as a cucumber "the whole shop, Jonny" Well I just stared at him for a few moments waiting for him to say I'm only joking, but all he could do was smile at me " go on then let's have some Flumps Jonny" . I replied get us a carrier bag then "ok" Tigger said so he went in his kitchen and brought one out. I always did running around for Tigger I wasn't a lackey boy or anything

I just Never minded cos his bike was ace a red Rayleigh Grifter there wasn't another like it on the estate I loved riding that bike and he knew it he saw my weakness I guess he sent me on all sorts of errands on that bike throughout that summer!

So, there I am parked bike up outside Geoff Hall's shop didn't need a lock in those days and walked in calm as you like and stared out the jars of sweets behind the counter! "Morning Jonny Boy, " said Geoff in a cheerful manner always called me that for some reason Jonny was not enough for him as most called me. "and what can I do for you today young man"? he asked with a cheesy grin.

So, I just blurted it out "ermm I want Flumps" I replied "there two a penny you know? special offers this school holiday," Geoff said calmly "well Giz em all then"?

So, He looks at me in disbelief! "and asks "them all"? but that's going to cost you £1.50" "yeah I know Giz em then" I said. anyway, he had two jars in that day and I took them both "We're camping out Mr Hall" I said "were camping out the whole six-week holidays so might be back for some more an all "

"Well don't eat them all at once or else you'll rot your teeth, young man," said Geoff and that was to be the beginning of our adventure that school summer holiday. I just remember feeling a real sense of liberation of freedom really, think we all did away from our parents a whole 6 weeks ahead of adventure lay before us,

So, I leaves the shop and climb onto The Red Grifter God I loved that bike and everyone used to stare at me because it was the only bike of his kind on Flanshaw at the time, it honestly made me feel a king riding past all my friends posing, anyway back at Tigger's me our Mick and Tigger laid on his backyard lawn sweating in the sun staring up at the clear blue summer sky, and we ate them Flumps we ate them until our bellies nearly burst.

So, the summer of 1979 was well in full swing now myself Our Mick and Tigger were managing to survive on rations of baked beans hot dogs and sometimes if we were lucky we would sneak into Tigger's house at night when his parents were asleep and pinch a bit of bacon or sausage or both! that in itself proved to be quite a mission having to open the door slowly carefully and really quiet in the early hours without waking his mum and dad up! problem is when everything is quiet at night even twisting a door handle can sound as loud as a Jumbo jet or something anyway after sneaking it we accomplished our mission and sneaked quickly and quietly into back garden and cooked ourselves baked beans and bacon we always managed to burn the camping tin pan set his dad had bought us though! but the food tasted lovely just remember sat their warm summer early morning the grass beneath us a bit cold the morning sparrows and starlings tweeting away and the sun just rising above the horizon! great times absolutely one of the best times of my life was that summer of 1979! one morning we were all laid there talking about girls we fancied at school I won't name names here but let's just say the discussion got pretty intense and strictly man talk folks.
and so, it was we had managed so far four back-breaking weeks with hardly ever having had a bath or anything Ok maybe once or twice but not often it's safe to say we stunk like a skunk and looked like a Miner,

Anyway, one morning we bumped into another friend as we had decided to go a morning mooch we saw Shaun Allen and Kev Lund they too had slept in a tent not as long as we had done but that's by the by, anyway one morning as me our Mick and Tigger were crawling the streets on a summer morning looking for milk and fresh orange to pinch off taffys milk float,
we saw them both walking down Wasdale we met up and did the usual small talk then Shaun asked why don't we all go up to Saint Paul's church and spook ourselves ! this needs to be explained before I go any further well what it was with us a lot on Flanshaw we had a thing about Saint Paul's churchyard being spooked and the reason we thought it was, was because in the tower if you stood a certain way and looked up at you

would be able to see two bright shiny eyes looking down at you ! now looking back, it was either a kestrel nest or light reflecting off something or other lol but anyway we were kids remember? it was none of those things it was obviously a demon waiting to pounce on us or an evil ghost that could not rest !! but this particular morning as we walked up Saint Paul's hill we got half way and when suddenly Shaun Allen stopped in his tracks.

"look over there," he said in a bit of an alarmed tone of voice "where"? we all asked, "there look there's a woman in a black dress walking around that tombstone!" "Where? we all asked ducking down by the York stone wall surrounding Saint Paul's School. "there look closely " Shaun said, and we did and we saw what he saw a Lady in a Black Dress seriously walking around this old tombstone with her head lowered down and as if what we were looking at was a sort of moving picture some kind of projection animation etc. well we ran we ran like the clappers down the hill all of us running like our lives depended on it and we kept running an all!

right up until we got to the Chippy on Batley road where we only stopped cos I was knackered and needed a breather. so, we discussed we debated all the way back to our tents was it, or wasn't it? either way, none of us slept wink that night instead we went a nicked ourselves a few pints of milk and some fresh orange even got a dozen eggs and cooked omelette's in the morning to try and forget the experience. That was the second Ghost I had ever seen the first back at Wilson terrace before I moved to Flanshaw. and I've never seen one since anyway later that week we all went back up there to look at the tombstone some Mary something or other was buried there 1876 frightening ey? so, we were edging ever so close now and near the end of the holidays and Tigger and our Mick were moving on to high school Tigger went to Thornes house our Mick was going to Eastmoor and I was to finish my last year at Saint Michael's it everything was about to change as our childhoods were reaching their conclusions.

And that school holiday 1979 did sadly, in the end, turn out to be pretty much the last I saw of me best pal Tigger. Mainly because he was moving onto high and I was still in middle school we just naturally drifted apart and as September came around the world moved on and we all went back to school.

I was now in my 4th and final year at Saint Mick's and our Mick and Tigger starting their first third year in High School! don't get me wrong we still hung out together but it there was to be one last adventure we would go on together and that was half term his mum and dad took us on holiday to Cleethorpes! for the week and that was where I met my first girlfriend, my first love, I never forgot her kept a photo she gave me but the years went by and it somehow vanished.

her name was Wendy she was beautiful! an absolute stunner slim tall much taller than me the same age but much taller. and Tigger got with her sister Carol, we met at the arcades one night and it went from there really back of the arcades we had a snog or two we met them for the last few days of the holiday I liked her so much that when we got back home I somehow plucked up the courage and managed to go visit her in Mexborough after a few chats from phone box I went with a few school pals, Mark Chapman and Shane Storie , we did this a few times and we would all hang out by the canal locks them playing gooseberry while I sat kissing and cuddling Wendy as you do.

I suppose. Shane and Mark came over mostly out of curiosity really but also to just simply get away from Wakefield for the day now you have to remember something here I was 13 years old and it was deemed safe back then to allow your kid to travel on a train with no adult supervision over 60 miles round trip and get home at 8 pm in the evening dark nights an all it was normal though your kids were not kids unless they were out of their parents to face. it's just how parents rolled back then seriously, and that's pretty much all there is to say about 1979 a fantastic year full of ups and a few downs mostly the fact I lost my best pal and lost touch with Wendy too cos of the distance and fact we really were just kids ... but times were changing the world was changing and I was now the ripe old age of thirteen!!

New Decade new start new year started with Pretenders Brass in Pocket and ended with Saint Winifred's school choir singing about a grandma!!!

yep, that's how diverse music was at the time ... So, where was I our Phoenix youthy had just opened its doors John Walker Godis our Mick Jeff Hudson John Ogdon Richard Ogdon Sue Heslop Daz Plews Alison Plews Andy Williams Andy Heslop Lindon Heald Mark Chapman Shane Storie Colin Godfrey Shaun Allen Kev Lund ... Steve Lund Lee Whiteley Sometimes his brother Mick Whiteley Ian Barraclough and Sometimes but not always I would also bump into my old pal Tigger but mostly the others I mention. Always remember Thursday and Sunday nights 7 pm stood outside in the yard waiting for Bob Walker the owner to open the old red wooden doors we would stand in the car park swapping stories of Our Music knowledge I for one had started to smoke and would always buy a few separates off Frank Perry from his Shop on new Scarborough!

Always bought a quarter of Kop Kops or sugar peanuts from him too. and then would make the journey along Batley road and head for the youth club the song from the 70's Suzy Quattro if you can't give me love was always the song the DJ would play first when I walked through its doors. I would pay my ten pence admission to Jean Walker who would sit there behind a table as you walked in always had a smile for us all did Jean and once she was paid I would walk into the big hall where table tennis tables were a new game had arrived that year too called it Space invaders and this was situated to the left of me and also to the left of the telly room door dead in front of me was the main hall which housed table tennis tables to the right of this was the main door into the dark but brightly lit dark disco room red green and blue lights flashing away to the music ! long 70's flowered curtains hanging from its windows never forget to hear these songs a few popular songs even though they were out in 1978 the DJ at the time Norman Rennles would play them all the same Suzi Quattro and this one too the drummer man by tonight great times were Phoenix youth club it brought all the kids in the neighbourhood together a real sense of belonging a community of like-minded youth brought together under one roof ! to dance the night away or watch the colour telly in that famous telly room !!! also in here was a tabletop pinball machine in the corner and I would play this often were Bob walker the owner would keep the high scores on record and award us with sometimes free admission or a pint bottle of blackcurrant juice or orange juice ! And that's pretty much the way I saw it be honest. a new Era if you like? Where Music was changing so quickly, mostly for the better but also some really crap an all! it was as though the whole world wanted that change a new direction to be being politicized

CND (Campaign for nuclear disarmament) was a member of this at the ripe old age of 12 and 3 quarters ! the Russians were coming or so we were told the cold war in full swing we also had new toys to play with new gadgets to be owned in the not too distant future games consoles ATARI massive absolutely massive , but there was, in fact, one console out before Atari and that was a console called grandstand we had it back in seventies, I can't remember where we got it from but it was an absolutely amazing experience to plug it in the back of our black and white telly and play pong ! all the family were gathered around the telly to witness it fire into action!

Our Mick and I thrashed the hell out of it! but I always threw teddy out the pram when I lost though this was one of many reasons I and many others realized the world was about to change there was a massive influx in new gadgets better than before stronger faster bit like the 6 million-dollar man I suppose and so it began I remember new year's eve 1979 we had a proper Xmas tree back then and I remember how we all as a family felt that bit extra excited as the clock ticked over to 12 am ! the world went wild that night parties all over the place up and down the country massive absolute massive parties big fireworks a proper celebration fitting of a new decade

So, 1980 was pretty much a year of hope and change and that life we were told would be much better than the worn out old seventies had been and that these decade gadgets were to make our lives much simpler women were told they wouldn't need to work as much and everyone felt optimistic about the future!

Back on Flanshaw, most of us kids were about to hit that magical age thirteen and become teenagers I spent a lot of time in the '80s at the Phoenix youthy used to love buying pop and crisps from the Phoenix canteen Jean Walker used to serve everyone with a big smile! and we would hang out in there talking all things punk rock or whoever was in the news or on top of the pops at the time there was this strange sound coming around with synthesizers and electronic keyboards Gary Numen Kraft work etc.

And I have to admit was grabbing my attention! This was 1980 folks a fresh start I suppose I was going to have to embrace it whether I liked it or not there was a strong wind of change blowing and I was slap bang in the middle of it , besides I liked space invaders that's if I could ever get Godis off it, he always hogged the space invader machine no one ever got the chance to beat his high score as he bloody hogged it all time so, I would usually spend my pennies on the pinball machine or a game of table tennis in the main hall with John Routledge And John Ogden .

And the girlfriends we met mine was a good-looking lass called Karen our Mick copped off with her mate Cheryl she also was a cracker and we somehow always ended up being dragged in the telly for no other reason than to have a snog because it was dark and quite too and everyone else was either in the disco or trying to get Godis off the space invaders. So yes, I had a few more months to go before I left Saint Michaels and moved up to big school Eastmoor High! we didn't really do much of note towards the end of Saint Micks! I do however remember our last sports day !! the teachers played rounders with us all and we actually beat them!! I was reminded by Godis the other day that Mr Whelan was a fast runner! and despite his size come to think of it he actually was, what else of note was there to remember in our final days of Middle School? well, not a lot really as I said one thing stands out though were the teachers they suddenly began treating us like young adults and stopped talking down to us as they used to do that was a strange one.

And so, our final day came and remember having my white tatty school shirt plastered with my mate's names wishing me luck and sadly after that I never saw or heard from them again as some went to Thornes House and others went to Eastmoor. yep come to think of it. it actually was a brutal ritual leaving school and a tad heartbreaking to boot.

 I mean lifelong friendships we had made over the years were crushed and decided by some snotty nosed god knows who telling us where we had to be educated next sort of thing, this practice is inevitable for sure but it's the brutality of it I'm trying to express here. And even if we still lived close by we all seemed to go our separate ways

Anyway, that aside along came the summer holidays 1980 this time around it was spent getting to look the part of those new heroes of mine madness I had an old suit I had bought off the second-hand market in Wakefield and it actually fitted alright for a thirteen-year-old kid! black it was and I felt a bit like a gangster wearing it, me and John Routledge once spent a weekend walking around Flanshaw spotting old men with *trilby hats and asking.... well more like begging actually to give is their hats cos they were trilby hats folks we simply could not be mods without them, so pretty much as I said most the holidays were taken up hunting down old granddads but to be honest as fun as all that sounds things were becoming to feel a bit stale, to be honest cos you got to remember I was now thirteen years old and most of us had done pretty much everything there was to do as a child but we want children anymore we needed a bit more than just Evil Knievel on a Saturday morning or playing Curby on our street stickleback and catfish fishing like the good old days, and something had to change me Godis our Mick John Walker we sort of hung around the Flanshaw streets kicking tin cans hands in our pockets we did this regularly and seriously lacking something to do boredom isn't the word here.*

John Walker Spent a lot of his spare time painting His Bedroom black and he designed an awesome mural of the late great Sid Vicious on his wall as too and we were that bored he had the brainy idea well actually a very clever idea come to think of it of dying his and Godis's hair leopard skin colours. Amazing it looked it too, Seriously to be fair to him he did a grand job there I have to admit cos John was a bit of an artist still is and has some pretty nice tattoos these days etc. so anyway, where was I ? oh yes so, we were a tad bored running out of ideas what to do next punk was out of my life for the time being although the spirit of it never left me, I was how do I explain this? on the surface a mod but my heart and soul was still punk !! still is to this day!

as for Godis and John and even our Mick to a certain extent were still dressing punky our Mick was still into the boomtown rats and even won once won a 45-single record at the Sirdar Xmas Disco 1979 with Daz Arnell

Chapter Eight

Sidings Batley

I was, in fact, told the other day he still works there but yeah, our Mick managed to look scruffy but it sorts of came to him naturally anyway! we all had to work at it! so yeah back on topic I was a bit of an odd one out really but was it me being original? or was it them? who knows? and anyway they both looked a bit damn cool to be fair to them I felt deep down a secret envy cos in my head I was willing to ditch madness and the mod thing if my mum had allowed Wack to do my Blonde Locks Leopard skin !! well not being funny or anything here but mine would have looked the best well cos I am natural blonde of course, Can you sense the green-eyed monster coming out of me here?

So, the street games were drying up as I reached my teens, everyone I had had the pleasure of growing up with was now looking for something different which brings me on to my cousin Judith, think she had just passed her test this year and she was visiting mum.

"Jonny," she said to me whilst sat in our living room watching Swap Shop and Noel Edmund's Taking Phone Calls, "yes Judith What? " I asked "I'm working in a nightclub in Batley now called sidings and was wondering seeing as your mum tells me you're bored all time how would you and your mates like to come over Friday night they have a teeny disco there " she asked. "yeah go on then I'd love to Judith" I excitedly replied "well I'll come over next Friday then and pick you up you can only bring three mates with you though cos my car only takes five" she said. " yeah ok Judith" I replied.

Our Judith had a white Vauxhall Viva back then quite an ugly looking car, but wow could it motor, very fast car it was and she drove it that way too, anyway all that week I was thinking about this Disco in Batley our Mick and Tony Everett came with us too. I just remember pulling up outside I wore straight denim jeans my Parker with madness badges all over it and me trilby hat. our Mick in his jeans and PVC leather jacket with boomtown rat's badges all over it and Everett in his jeans Monkey Boots and a plain white t-shirt Godis And Wack also joined us not long after this and Godis Wore his red leather bikers jacket docks and jeans and wack wore black leather coat with Sid painted on it Godis was never allowed in though Cos of his age still heroically made the journey with us he would sit outside on the dry stone wall waiting for us.

So, we pull up outside in our Judith's Car and it was dark cold windy night as I remember! because Batley was always windy anyway cos it was full of hills! we used to say that's all it had was Hills and taxi's and we were right an all.

So out of the car I took a deep breath cos I was nervous Batley beginning of the decade felt like a faraway land anyway so we climb out of our Judith's Viva and onto the cobbled streets climbed the steps to the double doors music was playing loud, much louder than saint micks disco an all. loudest I'd ever heard before. the specials were playing their song do nothing as we walked through the door and paid our 50p admission just remember seeing these strange creatures dressed in eighties colourful fashion burgundy tank tops and white granddad shirts clean chino kegs clean-cut kids with clean faces all staring at us cos they were all into that disco nonsense and trendy fashion crap.

Japanese boy was playing now don't get me wrong it was alright and catchy tunes but didn't go down so well for me it just seemed as though Batley had completely forgotten the punk era few years before or they never even had it in the first place.

There were a few skinheads pottered about too which are another story I will get to later, but for now where were we? are yes Sidings, so we walk in and we sat in this sofa on the far-left corner it had a wooden shelf over the top of it which if you leaned over you could see the dance floor and DJ box and the red green and blue lights flashing while the mirror globe on the ceiling would swirl around reflecting onto the polished wooden floor below. Japanese Boy by Aneka was playing.

We walked in there looking all cool and stuff and Batley Folk were not used to seeing strangers in town! especially punk rocker or cool mods from Wakefield. anyway, we sit down me Everett and our Mick we didn't make any effort to talk to anyone really. don't get me wrong we were friendly but distant because of the unfamiliarity of it all if that makes sense? and besides, we were Wakey boys we were too cool to be anything else. It felt a bit like Clint Eastwood walking into an out of town bar in the wild west films on the telly when curious heads would turn sort of thing!!

obviously, we made the situation worse with the fact we were all dressed as scruffy punks really and I dressed in unfamiliar Mod clothes. Anyway, as the night progressed my heavy metal worshipping cousin Andrea came over and sat with us all brought us some crisps and pop and we sat chatting or should I say shouting into each other's ear lugs over the crap disco music, well she asked what we thought of it and we said yeah, it's alright. and her friends also came sat with her Dawn another called Joanne another called Andrea who was also a mad headbanger like our Andrea and also present was a lass called Cally Who Godis later became her boyfriend. all good-looking girls all wore the 80's Rar Rar skirts sexy as hell I tell yeah.

my cousin Andrea wore this black scruffy looking Biker leather jackets with a denim waistcoat over top of it, it had sowed on cotton badges of motor heard Judas priest etc. bloody headbangers I thought, oh aye and they smelled of dead bodies an all embalming fluid and Andrea My Cousin used to have joss sticks too and smell of them well they made me feel sick.... bloody hippies I thought, and so our first night at Sidings went down well Judith me cousin who had made it all happen walked across to us with her car keys in hand and asked if we had enjoyed it? we shrugged our soldiers and in that teenage voice and manner and cool as you like replied yeah it was alright Cuz...so she walked us out the door into the fresh air still windy and blowing a bit of a Gale an all. we walked across the cobbled road climbed into her white Vauxhall Viva and made our way home back to

Flanshaw. on the way home,

we chatted about which Girls we fancied we couldn't wait to go back there the following week.

Anyway, I also told me to make John Walker AKA Wack when I got back told him sat in his black painted bedroom one night. yeah, I told him about how they were all weird over there and wore funny clothes. cos obviously as punks we did not do we? he too along with Godis Joined us going over there after that... but because there were five of us Godis Everett Wack Me and Our Mick we no longer could go in our Judith's Car so we would all make the short walk over the grazzy field along left side of tennis courts and then would cut through a small gap in hedge top of Grazzy field that gap in the hedge seemed to have been there for eternity!

Anyway, it led us to the 422 Batley bus stop which was over the road from the horse field and at the time where eddies fun fair parked up annually... And so here we were 1980 which was also to be the start of my high school years and also the start of new adventures over in our new playground Batley.

So, the following Friday Night Came along a lot of talk had come and gone over that night at the Sidings Nightclub. mostly centred around the girls we had met the previous week. we were awakening sexually thirteen going on twenty-one sorts of thing. more testosterone pumping around in us lads than a Ferrari driver on the final lap of an f1 race! so, Friday night came and were all stood on Batley road waiting for the 422 to show up stood there asking one another for a swallow off each other's regal king size etc. there was a saying back then which was "Giz a swallow of that"? and if you asked for a match the reply would always be "yeah my Arse your face"

I always had a nervous feeling in my stomach before going to the Sidings don't know why or anything maybe it was to do with the clothes I wore and being centre of attention as all of us seemed to be see it came with the territory being a punk and a mod I tended to drift from mod to punk for a while in those days and to come later in my story is when I decided to go the full mod thing!

Anyway, that was ok in Wakefield to be different, but Batley was different...full of disco heads and odd-looking skinheads. I felt a bit like a goldfish in a bowl being watched on by curious eyes etc. as cool as it was also always a bit unnerving for me too. Mainly for me personally as it felt like we were at the other end of the world or so it seemed, six whole miles away felt like six hundred in those days.

Anyway, we spent all the journey telling Godis an Wack how awesome it was and about all lasses there that came over and spoke to us the week before so we get to the Sidings the Wakey Gang the cool ones had landed and whilst heroic Godis sat outside we walk in through the door paid our 50p and sat in that corner with the wooden sofa again tainted love was playing and the room was full of the usual disco heads and bright shiny blue red green disco lights flashing away too. we sat there and our Andrea brought us pop crisps I never once or did any of us ever go to the bar for drinks Nah we were too cool for that nonsense we just sat and posed in the corner while the Batley lads all disco freaks would dance most the night trying with their whole heart and souls to impress the birds dressed in their white granddad shirts and Burgundy tank tops and chinos nonsense,

It was all a bit sad really and then there were the skinheads an all a few of them hung out there dressed in Fred Perry shirts jeans and docks looked quite intimidating really but never phased us wakey boys !!! and there seemed to be resentment building up with the skinheads from Birstall the atmosphere was made worse cos we were all sick of Godis being refused entry for being a year too old we all walked out in protest it somehow though gave us street cred in front of those Batley girls we were controversial and a tad arrogant and I suppose looking back I think they enjoyed that bad boy thing ,so weeks past I ended up for a short time with a lass called Joanne but eventually got with a girl called Christine and we began to hang out every weekend here on the Healy over in Batley. my brother Mick went out with her mate Amanda and Godis ended up with that lass I mentioned earlier Cally. we'd hang out on street corners smoking regal king size kissing cuddling love tapping that kind of thing, one day we even all decided to sleep out over there which I will come onto shortly.

Meanwhile back in high school

Eastmoor High was going really well new school new uniform new friends I was in a class called 3m my new teacher was called Mr Shearn and this is the way they worked out how clever you were back then was like this Eastmoor high school spelled the word (Bermuda) B being the brainiest set and E next and so forth I was in 3M which meant the system classed me of average intelligence and those early days at high school were awesome , I felt so grown up being in high school and those first cold windy autumn months catching the 114 Eastmoor bus to school each autumn morning top of Flanshaw hill was awesome remember walking up the hill heading towards Eskdale then on to the hill groups of us in our little gangs smoking regal king size and showing off the new artwork on our rucksacks debating whether to walk to school risk being late , or being able to buy a pack of 10 regal king size ! these were the hard choices we had to make each and every morning growing up often, I would bunk off school walk down the hill with me mate Hobbit and go buy a pack of 10 regal king size from the Spar at Thirlmere road shops I had befriended a lass on our street she had moved in the previous week, they moved next door to Mrs James's where Mr.'s James mum used to live the one who used to give me 50p to go to the shop for her every Saturday morning remember?

well this lass was called Joanne Burnett, and she had a brother Kirk the one who fell out of the tree he was a hell of a character they lived with their mum and dad her mum was a beautiful woman so down to earth laid back came across as a wise woman who seemed to have seen it all done it all kind of thing ,and always spoke her mind said it as it was always had a cig in her mouth as I remember too , and looked the spitting image of her daughter Joanne her dad was much more like Kirk small in stature slim almost boney looking he wore a tash that looked like Omar Sharif as I remember and wore worn out tired looking jeans he owned a red Ford Pontiac massive American muscle car with a confederate flag on the roof it was a beauty car stood out from the rest on our street although we did have a family who owned a TR7 once . so anyway, the Pontiac a dramatic tale to tell about that later in my story when I bunked off from school it was always either at me mates Everett or at Joanne's which was more or less opposite our house a daring thing to do considering. because when I was there I used to take a sneaky look through Joanne's living room curtains and often saw my mum in our garden or talking at the gate posts with one of the neighbours whilst it was a bit of a crazy thing to do really bunking off opposite our house. I never once got caught though but more on my school days later.

Chapter Nine

Those Magical CB Days

So, 1981 was upon us and there were many things happening around this time so many technological changes too! my mate Jonna Lindley invited me round his one night to dying to show me something, so I turned up at his, Jonna was a swarve looking dude looked Italian naturally dark skinned and had a way with the girls! I thought he had invited me round to show off his new bird or something lol. but nope in his bedroom side of his bed was this radio and it was blurting out voices lots of different voices young old I just remember standing at his door and asking him "so come on then Jonna what's this like? " he sat me down and said "this dial takes you up and down channels this dial will swr it "in other words tune it in for those not savvy." This is my trial it's hanging out my bedroom window at moment but I'm going to screw it to one of mum's biscuit tins and stick it in my loft! "slow down Jonna" I said, "ooooh so what does this thing actually do though?" I asked in an excitely curious tone of voice. " well it lets you talk to people Jonny Birds everything! Jonna replied coolly as you like!

the thought of speaking to girls sounded appealing to me "Show us then " I said. and so, he did he twisted the channel dial onto the number 14 pressed in his mike and said in a cool not his own usual voice " 14 a lady breaker" loads replied. " yh you got a lady breaker smash a window good buddy "I asked him "What's that mean?" he replied "watch and learn Jonny".

So, I did I sat there and listened to Jonna chat to loads of lasses on the CB that night. and it turned out a long one too as his mum worked at Lyons Bakery so throughout that summer we more or less had the house to ourselves all-nighters every night and every weekend until school holidays were upon us and then it was more or less 24/7

This was the new thing to be into! it was massive it meant we no longer needed to use our mums phones at the bottom of the stairs on those wooden/glass cabinets anymore !and a 10p box begging to be filled and if you tried sneaking a freebie your mum would shout even before you had put the receiver down don't forget to put 10p in the box, Jonny, nope we had this radio that once wired up to an aerial let you speak for the price of your parents electric a fair trade if you were a parent back then as phoning people was and still is an expensive past time,

I'll be honest most of this year was taken up talking on this new CB Radio! it was an amazing thing to have! everyone got one I got one the whole world seemed to have one! it was as big as the thing we call the internet today it was the pioneer of Facebook and all things social media it preceded all of that! it truly was the Daddy of communication of the time, Facebook today is pretty much its offspring I'd say! although no way as good as that old CB, unlike Facebook you only get to type to people and for that one reason alone brings out the worst in some as they hide behind their keyboards often with an attitude, not all mind but some do, whereas CB radio was awesome it was you the mike and your personality booming over the airwaves ! it was awesome the world after 1981 suddenly felt much smaller because of this little metal box sat at the side of most of our beds it changed a whole generation ! believe it or not, people met and married on these boxes and I'm guessing some are still with each other even today
!!!

so here I was a year into high school still into the Mod Ska music craze and now this awesome and strange craze CB to add to the fun of it all, strange in the fact we could actually talk to just about anyone anywhere within say a 25-mile radius, to begin with until you upgraded and then you could reach more folk, Complete strangers! Mostly girls, of course, they were called lady breakers and our goal as lads almost every time we switched on our Rigs was to find and talk to as many of them as we could teenage hormones I guess it consumed me! it consumed everyone especially me *mates we all had to have one and I wasted no time in getting mine, I bought Jonna's old one from my wages working for GK Hall and boy did that job come in handy just as the CB radio craze started.*

He bought a bigger one from old Jack Lingwood at bottom of Westgate, a chaser 500 had little green and red led lights at the front, and as you spoke they would flash from left to right.

Amazing bit of kit was that. Jonna it seemed was pretty much a stay at home geek looking back. Well, his mum worked the night shift at Lyons Bakery and as I mentioned earlier in my story this gave him the keys to the house basically after 7 pm until 7 am the following morning we would tinker about with electronic odds and sods he was always tinkering around with stuff was Jonna. we once attempted to hotwire his mom's home phone and take it off the grid. We spent almost a week every night trying to work that little puzzle out but when a few sparks began flying about we put that idea to bed. Anyway, my Rig was a Midland 40 channel light blue in an appearance at the front and the same colour all around! silver buttons switches at the front and at night time dimly lit my bedroom with its white led light that lit up the signal meter.

So That's pretty much what I got up to in 1981 CB Radio! first time I used it I only spoke with Jonna who lived just behind me on Eskdale Rd. Well, it was so weird owning this thing and for ages, I would not really talk to anyone bit shy I guess in the same way I was when I moved onto Keswick all those years ago !!! it really was as weird as it got. And you have to remember before this to talk to anyone meant having to put 10p in my mum's wooden phone box at bottom of stairs but that was totally different to having a CB! in so far as ok on a phone no one else could listen or jump in your conversation!

Having A CB certainly changed all that! everyone could hear you and many would break in on the channel to talk. Made a lot of friends on that old battered up radio in my bedroom. Have to say I also made a lot of enemies too, mainly through playing sex pistols over the breaking channel while folk were trying to get out or falling out with someone who liked a girl I liked teenage stuff really.

Once I got the hang of the lingo and got my confidence up I spent every moment available to me on it and would regularly spend all night sessions chatting away with anyone or everyone. Summer 1981 was fast approaching! and soon the 1978 movie convoy was out at the cinema it had a bit of a revival once the CB craze was in full swing! terrific movie and the song too by C. W. McCall and Chip Davis that was in the charts too! The song's success helped start a fad for citizens band (CB) radio. in the UK and it took off like a rocket or a Smokey bear chasing down one of those big bad truckers !!! after everyone had seen the movie of course!!

Massive absolutely massive it's hard to express in words how big CB was on Flanshaw and Wakefield as a whole really. I remember once looking out of Jonna's window and over towards Lupset on the horizon and just remember seeing Twigs as they were called Ariel's if you're not Savvy!! Well anyway, Twigs of all lengths and sizes on just about every rooftop on Broadway! and same story to tell on Flanshaw I also remember mum and the neighbours complaining of hearing my voice coming over their tellys, because unless you put that Twig in a good spot or SWR it in with an SWR meter a sort of little metal box with dials on the front it meant your signal would shoot all over shop! and that created all kinds of problems for my mum with our neighbours complaining to her about my voice coming over blankety blank and Dallas not only next door but most the street an all. Well, that was until I realized you could buy special low pass frequency filters From Jack Lingwood's that shut all that interference off suddenly everyone was my mum's friend again oh the days the '80s were a great time to be alive!

Summer 1981 and so much going on both at home and at my new school Eastmoor High also me mates and me were all still travelling to Batley for the Sidings Disco ! and causing mayhem over there with the local lads ! not the girls just the lads , well for some odd reason they got a tad jealous cos us wakey boys were stealing the local talent but look we were not looking for trouble it just came to us honestly,so back in Wakefield me Godis Whack Our mick Jonna plus loads more to mention were happily talking away on our CB'S. In the beginning, it all seemed to be about talking to each other until then we realized there was a new craze that added a whole new dimension,

the idea of an Eyeball well this basically meant if you got chatting to a nice sounding lady breaker on there you would then arrange to meet up after talking to them for a short while. The usual meeting place was Flanshaw library just past my old school Saint Mick's on the Flanshaw road it used to be on the corner where the Flanshaw road met Dewsbury road! and there would be a low wall we would sit on waiting in the hot summer sun for our on-air romance to turn up! have to admit some of the

*girls I met turned out to be not quite what I anticipated though my tactics
I developed after much trial and error went like this*

*the sexy sounding girls were basically dragons and the rough sounding
girls absolutely hot and I learned the best way to avoid such
embarrassment in future was to tell them I would be wearing certain
jeans or a certain colour top that I actually was not, just so If in the event
of a disaster*

*I could make my get away with no harm or feelings hurt on either side if
they were dragons basically, Cruel yeah but look we were young and
sometimes that meant being cruel to protect your street cred. This little
trick worked I'm pretty certain the girls would do the same to me too
anyhow. Those eyeballs they were scary and filled you with adrenalin
going on them,*

*Well, what I mean is if it went bad it got the adrenalin rushing walking
past them hoping they would not recognize me, but on the other hand if
they were hot it got the testosterone and the hormones pumping. The
older end the ones who took it all seriously used to have chats on 32 low
band they spoke about all kinds of electronics chatting away about the
latest gadgets etc. which I incidentally used to enjoy listening to you
could learn a lot from these old guys well once I had upgraded my CB to a
Superstar 120 that was which offered loads more frequency bands than
that old 40 channel Midland well anyway they got together and came up
with a great idea instead of all these youths meeting up with one another
in middle of street why not give them a Disco to go to instead where they
could meet their future wives in a safer environment I suppose. and so, it
came to pass the CB Eyeball Disco was born! the first one I can remember
was held at the Roundhouse on Newton bar Leeds road I used to go here
with Jonna more than anyone else and we would call for Gunsight Neil
Greenwood if any of you know him! a nice lad was Neil Still being. in those
days, he was a well what I called a sissy band Duran Duran! they had a
song in charts hungry like the wolf and unfortunately for me my mate
Jonna Liked em an all!! Neil was short thin and I remember he always had
his hair all wavy like Simon L Bon lead singer of Duran Duran he paid a
fortune having it flashed with blonde streaks but he certainly knew how to
pull the birds did Neil IL give him that much.*

*Jonna on the other hand never did dye his hair he was natural black and
natural tanned and looked Italian and myself? well not much to say about
me really, well look I was a scruffy punk/mod of Flanna ok?*

I wasn't and couldn't bring myself to be a Duranny not a chance in hell even if it meant forfeiting the chance of a lovely girl I had principles and stuck to them end of.

So yeah, where was I? oh yeah so me and Jonna would call for Neil Greenwood we would wait for ages while he did his hair in the mirror enduring the sounds of Rio in the background as he did his hair ritual and then we, d set off to the roundhouse calling along the way for his mate Tony another good mate I got to know through CB he was albino was Tony a shade blind had bright white hair a great lad to know and always full of beans making jokes as we walked along peacock fields under the tunnel at Saint John's on our way to the roundhouse!

Happy days Folks, so whereas hearing Bowie in Tigger's bedroom and then getting into punk all those years ago and after hearing god save the queen on Godis's transistor radio and Punk music that had brought out the confidence in me.

CB gave me the chance to put my new-found confidence from all that to the test really. Cos the world was no longer confined to the Phoenix youth club anymore. where faces became familiar etc. CB was a whole new level as it now meant you met people you had never seen before or spoke with before and not a few minutes either it would last for ages, into the early hours most times even on school days which affected my ability to learn anything of importance. and usually more than not this gruelling nightly energy sapping ritual, would be carried out with complete stranger's and then other strangers would also break into your channel and this would create a sort of group chat banter and jokes flying around galore I tell yeah! did wonders for your confidence though! and soon after, these lads would also become your friends as everyone would turn up at the eyeball. And to find these strangers you spoke with came the invention of the CB Badge you would proudly wear an all cos it made noticing you at the Eyeball so much easier. Old Jack Lingwood at bottom of Westgate offered this service an old greyhaired bloke always wore a heavy knitted cardigan and smoked cigars like they were going out of fashion walking into his shop you could chew the Cigar smoke-filled air.

Anyway, think he charged around 5p he would look at u with his cigar in corner of his mouth one eye closed and ask so what's it to be today than younger? you'd tell him then he would get out this label machine and punch in your CB Handle onto it. And to this day I still remember the words on that old CB badge they were as follows.

"you have just met a sweet-talking ratchet jawing ear wigging barley popping super studding male/lady breaker and then your CB handle on the end of that lot. you could also pay 10p and have a glitter or day glow colour one that shone under the disco lights I stayed with a cheap white though me hated all that poxy disco nonsense and my handle was Mighty mouse or as some called me mighty mouth as I did gain a bit of a reputation on there as the wind up merchant and would also annoy the older folk by playing music over the channel 14 the breaking channel never played punk cos that would have given it away so instead I would play Duran Duran or Spandau Ballet as a decoy sort of thing to hide my person .. And my mate Jonna regularly got accused of my misdemeanours to his disadvantage.

Meanwhile back at School and the joys that was bringing and that Sidings Disco where Adam Ant was now gaining popularity and a song in charts that made number one Joe dolce shaddap your face these along with Specials too much too young among many more great songs were being played ritually each Friday night, and after many years listening to punk rock I had really began to develop an interest in teenage rebelling and causing as much chaos in the classroom as possible! Silly things really making farting sounds on my arm while inconspicuously trying to hide it from the teacher. Talking in class and cringe-worthy looking back at it now ignoring the teacher when telling me to stop disrupting the class etc. refusing to do any work and sitting at the back of classroom chair on its rear two legs vacantly staring out the second-floor window down onto the girls playing netball on the courts,

Think more than anything else this was down to the reputations we made for ourselves cos at school once you associate yourself with the clowns you became a clown yes do this even just once your reputation was set in stone the laws of association kind of thing , And It stuck with you and as much as you wanted to get away from it , it would never go away and the more you gained attention from your mates the cockier and more confident you got at being a complete Clown and it would stick with you and you had no way of escaping it no way whatsoever no matter how hard you tried to do the right thing ,
I remember at the time thinking to myself on many occasions Jon stop being a fool get your head down do the right thing for your mum make

her proud etc. but such was the pull of the popularity stakes at school and in that gang of ours I never followed my potential through or got my head down unfortunately , and even once or twice when I would sit on the bus smoking a regal kings on way to the Terminus stubbing it on the floor and thinking right today I'm going to do the right thing I'm going to change make those teachers who look upon me as a clown proud of me ,and I would turn up to class with good intentions I would I would sit at my desk with me chewed up battered old Bic Biro in hand my old scruffy rucksack on the floor under the desk with my dock Martin size nines resting on top of it had Specials Madness and Punk badges all over it

I had bought these from the fat man on wakey market I'd then open my book on a nice neat page the one I'm on about here the one on the right side with most paper under it for cushion effect and then I would look up shyly at the teacher trying not to get his/her attention but to see if he/she had noticed me and every fricking time he or she, our eyes would awkwardly meet and then I would be given that stare that expression which screamed at me come on then Holey what surprises you got in store for us today then? and I seriously would try my hardest to break that Rebellion in me, but those years of punk rock indoctrination by sex pistols and boom like a rocket going off on 5th of November one word or funny stare was all it took, i.e. a teacher sating wrong thing or a mate throwing a rubber at me or screwed up bit of paper or someone to make a twang sound by flicking his unbreakable see-through plastic Rule on the edge of the desk! and that's it I would be off again cos they made me act a clown I swear they did.

And as the week rolled by the school, fish and chips every day from Georges chippy and piles of homework out the way, Friday night arrived I had been at the Sidings Disco the week previous
Christine my girlfriend at the time had pulled me over to one side whilst we were sat in corner of disco quickly leaning over me ...more or less laid on top of me. I just sat there all embarrassed shouting over the top of that bloody awful song
" here this won't do you or me any good won't this! damage my cred for starters and yours an all, wanting to kiss a scruffy punk like me whatever will your mates think eh"? I Said with a sly grin and a twinkle in my eye and tongue in cheek she turns around looking at me a tad shocked and says "don't be daft I won't dare what you on about you? "so slightly disappointed that kiss wasn't coming anytime soon but not at all

surprised, and with a slightly hidden disappointment look on my face I simply could not hide she then asks me her voice piercing my ears hardly audible over the top of Japanese Boy and asked, well to me in a shy kind of dominant voice or maybe it just sounded that way because she was having to shout top of her lungs over that Aneka singing that crap song anyway, she screams down me lughole " Jonny if I can arrange it with my mate what would you say to us all kipping out next week like?" I thought eh? Kip out our lass? kip out where? And in a hopeful tone of voice with a heavy hint of sarcasm, I asked "I will if it means we. and paused at that point but she knew what I meant. yeah, that teenage testosterone rearing its head again.?

Fourteen and girls occupied my mind constantly what can I say? probably more than they should have but here I was not exclusive you know.? Most lads my age were going through the same thing, (Debbie Harry) was much to blame seeing her on top of the pops Thursday evenings hot as hell every teenage boy desire, not just mine either pretty damn certain of that so anyway, where were we? Oh yeah
Anyway, she replied to my sarcastic hopeful question, cryptically as all females do "Well You never know what might happen if you sort it and get your arse over next week and we'll see alright.?
So with those almost cryptic in nature and teasing words ringing in my ears for a week I had a mission a master plan was needed here thoughts of losing my virginity if I went about this right was in the stars so allnighters or midnight mooch to some came to my head as an idea, a sort of white lie we would tell our parents to get out of their clutches and be free for a night or two, The following week I attended school as usual I had a friend there who's dad worked in a shop on Flanshaw he was a tall muscular kid with curly fair hair and glasses was arguably the hardest in our school although no one ever knew for sure as he never put himself about really but a nice lad all the same so anyway I'm there one day sat round smokers corner by side of the gym deep in thought when he appeared from nowhere and said in a straight talk tone of voice "want to buy some cigs, Hooley?"
And as the week rolled along fish and chips every day and piles of homework accomplished Friday night would creep up and then it was time for The Sidings once more, Top of Batley road by the bus stop over road from horse's field waiting once more the 212 to pull up and off we went on our journey over the hill to Batley to meet once again those lovely kind

welcoming faces of the boys in Batley. Watching us suspiciously as we walked through those double doors and into our familiar spot in the corner of the dimly lit disco-lit hall

"no" I replied I've got 20 king size already mate. "no, he replies "I meant a lot of cigs mostly JPS but I have Benny and hedges an all so he opens his rucksack and wow never seen so many cigs in my life in one place. "where did you get these from "? I asked. "from my dad's shop and I need to get rid of them before I go home want to buy any? Well as it happens I was a bit loaded that particular day so I asks "how much"? "or give is 50p a pack so I did I bought over 200 off him cos the weekend was fast approaching and I had Batley on my mind Christine loved a cig or 3 an all and he said "if you need any more let me know but I will only supply to order in future cos it's too risky my dad will kill me.

And another thing doesn't go tell anyone Hooley it's more than my life worth to get caught with this lot my dad will publicly execute me and you wouldn't want that to happen to me, would you"? As it happens no I would not I thought as I mentioned he was arguably cock of school remember and I didn't fancy a public execution myself, to be honest, I replied and we left it there I said "nice one Mate" and we went our separate ways so I'm here with my rucksack full of dodgy tobacco loot and thinking wow what a bargain that was as 20 fags back then were approaching £1.50 I bout a mix 100 JPS and 100 B&h so pretty much the rest of the week was the usual mundane lessons we had a lesson I will never forget that there was a big teacher at school he was the horticultural teacher and I loved gardening me his name was Mr Simpson, AKA Daddy Plant Pot.

Remember me veg patch in my back garden in the 70s? well anyway he always made his lessons interesting and one day he took us to gardening in tool shed and brought out this massive lawnmower and announced "I need a volunteer" no one put their hand up including me and I sort of lowered my face to the ground as he asked the question anyway by doing so I brought the most attention to myself and he said " right you will do" "in his really broad Northern Accent to me "all I want you to do is this it's pretty simple young man it really is just pull that switch their lad that's the choke and pull this string here that will start the engine" well I did as he asked and it fired up loud as a Jumbo Jet it was I just stood there thinking no way am I operating this, for a start it was nearly twice the size of me . Anyway, he says "right I need the cricket pitch, mowing lad, I thought he was going to get me to mow around the tennis courts a simple task I thought at the time ,but no he asked me to mow the cricket pitch my instant reaction and I telled him an all "here sir If you make me push this up and down that, then the school will end up with a right cock eyed pigs ear of a cricket pitch cos I'm not tight confident pushing this and now you want me to mow our loved cricket pitch in a straight-line sir?. No soz Sir I can't do it I will mess it up to give the job to someone who's bigger and stronger than me." Mr Simpson simply smiled at me but he did as I asked and I never saw that bloody mower again after that, I was demoted to weeding I think he saw the fright on my face and the borderline child cruelty it was causing me.

I loved High School with my mates but more than anything I hated the lessons and the day to day stuff you know that thing learning but the comrade was second to none, I'll come back soon to more tales from high school but for now, I need to get back to Batley and the Sidings Disco,

So, Friday comes along and everything was set I had to hide those cigs from my mum they lay under the floorboards in my bedroom for over a week although I did and she never suspected anything I did sometimes nearly give the game away though when prizing floorboards open to sneak a pack but she never sussed me. Friday night it was the time I got unusually dressed a lot smarter than I normally would my jeans was not as ripped as me other ones I usually wore and I even got my mum to wash these an all.
A plain white tee shirt and a black Mohair jumper my tuxan red docks shined up like a new penny and I was ready for Batley or Batley was ready for me one or the other So I get outside garden says night mum IL see you in morning sort of thing she replied don't you be getting in any trouble do you hear?
I just turned my head and nodded no and that was it so I calls round for Godis our Mick was there an all getting changed and doing his hair all spikey in mirror and Godis was doing same Godis wore a menacing red leather motorbike jacket docks and jeans and out mick wore PVC trousers a black and red Denise the menace jumper black spiky hair he looked well he took ages though our mick to do his hair must admit it was always well

done though and smart in a scruffy punky kind of way. We were ready to rock n roll but Tony, where was he? We were meant to all be meeting up at Godis's but he was not there? We waited and waited and eventually, he turns up said he had a few jobs for his dad to do before he was allowed out. "Why didn't you call Godis," I asked least we would have known Everett, you dickhead. he just replied "I would have but our Julie was on it for ages I couldn't get her off it! Lies? Yeas probably,

So, there you have it four lean and mean Flanna boys ready to invade Batley once again we were running late though and needed to get shifty on so we run across grazzy field I had my rucksack with cigs in a bottle of clan dew Everett had bought earlier and we get to that gap in hedge at top of the field by tennis courts and 422 went flying past at breakneck speed.
Disaster we had missed the frikkin bus and not another for over half an hour, I was beginning to think this night was never going to happen and a sense of dread overcame me I did, in fact, have the Batley bus station phone box number as this was our means of communication back then, me Godis Everett our Mick we would often pile down to phone box bottom of s bends on Flanna with our pockets bulging with loose 2 pence pieces they had mostly saved mostly through course of the previous week from their dinner or bus fares to school, Myself ? well, I had earlier just landed a cushy number building the video store on Flanshaw with mick the spar man always had a bit of spare cash in my pocket as did Godis. We suggested we ring Batley Bus station phone box they hung outside of to let them know we would be late
Anyway, turns out I did not have any change that night nor did anyone else so even more reasons to be stressed so eventually nearly a full pack of JPs later and a throat rough as a bear arse the 422 eventually pulls up nearly 9 pm though but we made it finally and we headed over to sit down by the off-licence that was also in the bus station. Some passersby had a Tranny radio and it was playing Do Nothing by The Specials ... When at that very moment as the music drifted away from around the corner they all turned up Christine her mate Amanda, Our Andrea my cousin and her mate Andrea still headbangers and stunk of that bloody Petunia oil, but also a girl I had not seen before Amanda's younger sister Tracy think her name was well she copped off with Everett that night after many hours of persuasion by him and few white lies "where have you been? We

nearly walked off without you we waited by Nash for you" Christine asked me assertively she was dressed in a rar rar skirt and a leather coat and she looked amazing, So I Replies under my breath "well its cos of Everett" but I never actually completed pronouncing his name before he jumped over top of me and said

"it's because we ended up fighting with those skinheads that don't like us at Sidings Christine you know the ones "? So, I looks at Everett gone out and I'm thinking here you lying twat That's a Lie "But Everett carried on he could not stop himself, stop I thought, please just stop you twat but he proceeded "yeah, we beat em up the weirdos "Christine at this point looking all impressed as she stared across at me with a smile then she turns back to Everett and asks "how many were there then?" asked inquisitively " how many?" Everett replied "almost trying to buy more time to think of a good enough answer "oh erm ten there was ten of them Christine and all tooled an all up but we kicked the shit out them all " So who smacked who?" Christine asked curiously my Bird at this point looking mighty impressed "and who was was they ? do we know them ?" she asked " " no idea" says Everett

"Well I took out three of them, Mick took on three your Jonny took out three and big Godis took four out " So I'm sat there and I'm thinking to myself in my head hang on that's a crap lie you see Everett yes was usually a good spinner of yarns but had seriously messed this one up, he was never a Punk in a million years either but sure as hell tried, bless him

So, as you're reading this you do the Math you'll get my drift, and that's exactly What the girls did too it didn't take long to work that little pork pie out the Dickhead and all pretty much in unison shouts "shut up Everett Lying Twat" and began to laugh, but Everett he somehow backtracked and covered up the cracks and they still believed him god knows how he did it and to be quite honest I cannot remember but anyhow it worked... So that was that then as good as settled, suddenly we Flanshaw Boys looked hard as Nails and did our street cred no harm at all ... a lie, of course, cos in reality only Godis could handle himself out of us all and we relied on him a lot ...

Anyway, I want to complain always Funny when Everett told a Lie he always screwed it up 99% of the time though even if he did usually start it off convincingly.

So, the night started out pretty well talking about music amongst ourselves and deliberately avoiding that skinhead incident Earlier and then I said it if anyone wants a fag to see me as I opened my rucksack full of JPS and B&H the crowd went wild as the old saying goes and with a Volley of questions fired at me left right and centre where did you get these from Johnny can I have one? It was at this point I knew the night was going to work out well because even if I didn't lose my virginity I would die comfortably in a haze of tobacco smoke. So, what did we get up to then? Well apart from smoke our heads off and warm our bellies with that Clan dew of Everett's not that much really we walked around Batley all night drifting here and there and everywhere our girls holding on to our arms tightly as we mooched about the streets the Skinhead basher's they must have thought my boys a hero, far from the truth as you know anyway enough of that nonsense let's move on ,,so we decided to visit the churchyard down by the fire station to spook ourselves I also thought it would be a good time to get a bit closer to Christine as going somewhere like that she would almost certainly want to cuddle me and get closer than we normally would.

Ok, Look, call it a Teenage lads tactic or whatever you want to call it but anyhow it didn't work, quite a failure to be honest. Because she was hanging about with the lasses as I was the lads really so instead We sat telling ghost stories pointing out shadows under the moonlight that were obviously not ghosts but in the heat of the moment they were because we would convince ourselves there were, you get my drift here I'm sure you did this yourselves in your youth too.?

And It was also at this point I came to realize Christine was not having any of it her words from the previous week that something may happen between us didn't she had obviously forgot about or didn't want to bring it up because of her shyness but to be honest I too was shy an all and felt as guilty as she probably did , and although I did love her a lot, the Teenage Boy mind in me began thinking of all the reasons we cannot be together rather than why we could I shall come back to this later in my story though so, for now, read on

Ok, Look, call it a Teenage lads tactic or whatever you want to call it but anyhow it didn't work, quite a failure to be honest. Because she was hanging about with the lasses talking about us looking across and smirking as I was them with the lads really so instead We sat telling ghost stories pointing out shadows under the moonlight that were obviously not ghosts but in the heat of the moment, of course, they were because we needed to feel scared, you know what I'm getting at here I'm sure. We loved tapped one another but

And It was at this point I suddenly came to realize Christine was not having any of it her words from the previous week that something may happen between us didn't she had obviously forgot about or didn't want to bring it up because of her shyness but to be honest I too was shy an all, and although I did love her a lot, the Teenage Boy mind in me began thinking of all the reasons we cannot be together

So, the night apart from the little fact screaming in my face that I was not about to lose my Virginity anytime soon we strolled on Mooching around Batley Smoking those Fags like they were going out of fashion out of my old battered gloss painted sex pistols Sid swastika Khaki Rucksack Playing that game where you hear the sound of a car and before it appears and the driver catches you in his headlights you jump over a hedge or a wall to hide whilst it drives past. And then suddenly we are all back at the Bus station so cold it was an all Jesus it was February 81 and we were still in winter the cold biting on our cheeks we all cuddled up in a sort of mass ball really in the long dirty dusty old glass bus shelter and that moment as long as it lasted was a moment I shall never forget I really felt in my heart we were a gang forever a kindred friendship that would last on and on and beyond and into our adulthoods as we all did with our mates back then thinking this was to be forever and we would never fall apart grow up become old boring and leave each other and coincidently in the charts getting airplay was Rat Race By Specials which fitted the occasion perfectly

so that was my plan with Christine the next time I saw her was to do the terrible act of dumping her, so the night wore on we smoked more cigs that were rapidly disappearing from my Rucksack and that was pretty much it as all-nighters go the sun began to rise over the Batley skyline and my eyes began to lower as the tiredness began to affect me as well as a sore throat I had now developed and chesty cough we said our goodbyes I gave Christine a kiss and we were off back on the 422 to Wakefield.

Sunday back at home was mostly spent in bed mum asking why I was so tired me skipping past her quickly and then spending the next half hour or so in the bathroom cleaning my teeth trying to get rid of that tobacco breath, a week later and Christine came over to see me we spent a bit of time together but I ended it that day and that was that really, tears flowed but we moved on but that was the thing about childhood things came and went so quickly no time to stop and think just kept that ball rolling along . And it was these sorts of things that taught you about life we won we lost and we moved on no other way to handle situations like that as a kid apart from to learn a lesson even if it was the wrong one I made looking back on it now, cruel you might ask and yes it was but we were kids remember? And with leaving Christine really that was also leaving Batley and the sidings as at the time it felt too much of a hassle to bump into Christine at the sidings the following week so I stopped going my brother and Godis carried on for a while as Godis had met Cally over there and they were together quite a long time after our adventures had ended so abruptly so my brother and Godis would go over there not for the Sidings Disco but to Birstall to hang out with Cally Godis's girlfriend as for me I went back to school after a run of the mill summer holiday which had included my 14th birthday then the new school term was upon me and before I could blink 1982 was fast approaching and once it came life carried on pretty much the same as the previous year, The CB Radio was still in full swing and was my thing right now and that had many new adventures for me It became at the time the single biggest thing in my life I was constantly on it pretty much the way kids today are constantly on their smartphones only difference being is that CB was a sociable animal at school we spoke about it at home we spoke about pretty much everyone or anyone had one,

I began to also realize that school too was fast approaching the end and this year also was to be my 15th birthday and adding the months realized this was the age I would be leaving school an all and that summer of 1982 was unforgettable in so many ways Ebony and Ivory sang by Paul McCartney and Stevie Wonder was number one in May that year the mod scene still in flow but not as popular as it had been a few years previous and anyway for the first time in ages I seemed to have turned my back on music at this point in my life Punk was on his knees mods were too . many new distractions and new technology was taking hold one being the CB Radio and this was proving to be my biggest distraction,

My latest friend at this time was Jonna a cool and swarve sod he was six t pack to boot, always wore his shirt around his waist in summer and the lasses loved him and as I mentioned earlier we had many good nights sat in his bedroom on the Rig chatting away to girls far away as Hemsworth even and it taught us lessons in love and life about rejection too did that old CB and how to pursue the ultimate goal for a 14 year old flanshaw lad that being the pursuit of sex and losing one's virginity , getting involved in arguments with kids parents who did not take too kindly to me playing The Jam town called malice over the breaking channel when they were trying to get out on airwaves,

I really was a cheeky so an so and looking back on it all it's a wonder I did not get my nose displaced on a regular basis. But this CB was massive in the day it became a voice a way to express yourself to let the world know who you were and what you were about. albeit a luxury reserved only for the rich and famous our idols on that top 40 countdowns Sunday tea times finger on the pause button at the ready, and to suddenly be noticed and spoke about was a real ego boost back then because I don't know a kid on this earth who did not or does not want recognition growing up to develop their own persona to develop their own person etc. but this is exactly what CB Radio gave us as working-class kids growing up at the beginning of that wonderful decade of discovery the eighties.

Chapter Ten

A Video Shop

So it was about this time that Michael the spar mini supermarket manager on Flanshaw shops at Thirlmere collared me one day while buying an elephants foot, Michael was a middle-aged bloke small in stature short black hair wore a brown 70s looking leather jacket black nylon action slacks and smoked a pipe like it was going out of fashion stunk he did ,I can still smell that old pipe now whilst writing this, he wore his heart on his sleeve through a passionate ambitious man with a big heart, here and also turned out quite generous too as I was soon to find out, so there I was stood at the Deli counter buying a cream filled elephants foot from when suddenly he says to the lady serving me it "no charge"

I looked at him astonished and began to wonder why the show of generosity never had owt for free from a shop unless I lifted a few mojos now and then so it felt a bit strange getting summert for nowt, anyway he takes me to the side hand on my shoulder and pops the question "do you have one of those new video players Jonny"? I knew about these or should I say I was aware as they had been on telly on the ad breaks they let you watch a film at home instead of going to ABC, and I replied to him pretty much that thought really "yes I've heard of them but there really expensive me mam can't afford one but she's on about getting us one off slot telly man Mr. "I replied. "yes, that's the ones "replied Michael with a smirk on his face looking at me probably because of way I explained my answer god knows but anyway he says "how would you like to earn a few Bob helping me build a shop in my stock room next door "?
The stockroom he was on about was the little empty shop at the side of the Spar it had cardboard up on windows ever since time began and so I replied "yeah I will when do you want me"? "tomorrow Sunday if that's ok with your mum "?
So that was it I went home with cream cake smeared all over my mouth and told my mum, so Sunday came I walked in the empty shops because in those days shops didn't open Sundays I just remember him sat behind counter laid back relaxed and smoking his pipe "morning young man" he said "catch" and suddenly he threw over a packet of 20 regal kings I felt a bit unsure him knowing I smoked and he says don't worry I've seen you loads of times smoking you know it stuns your growth don't you ? he says . "aye so my mum said the one time she caught me " I replied so I was excited now he seemed a generous bloke did Michael and with that we walked next door he opens the door and there in front of me was a room full of cardboard and tins of various food old advertising posters strewn across the floor a real mess if I'm honest and so that was our first job cleaning the place out and transferring all his stock to back of Spar next

door once we had done this he showed me his plans he had wrote down I remember thinking wow he treats me like an adult and with respect he involved me and all the time whilst we built that place I felt like a partner of his or something, he made me feel wanted and appreciated it's just the way he managed folk he was very good at it ,so the days turned to weeks the weeks turned to months and I was loaded and screw by screw nail by nail it began to take shape , we can begin with the walls they had to be scraped filled and painted then he bought loads of wood paneling we then attached these to 2 by 1" batons on the walls first time I had ever used a drill and the first time I ever used a spirit level too I felt like a proper man now pencil behind my ear like Tigger's dad had one years before , we sat discussing the various stages of its construction and then onto the erection of a false ceiling we lowered it a good 12 inch with white plastic tiles suspended with thin wire at regular measured intervals along the ceiling that was hard work so age 14 now the summer was in full swing.

I spent many a dinner break outside the shop sat on what used to be a wall smoking my free Regal kings while also eating free food from his shop sarnies in wrappers, all the Elephants feet I could eat fresh Cream coming out of my ears it was, and he paid me a Fiver every weekend I was absolutely loaded and for those few months it took to build I never went short of anything new dayglo badges from fat man on the market even bought a new CB , I bought records , and sweets as many as I could eat, but not just me benefited either my mum did too because I would make sure we had food in cupboards at home an all, I absolutely enjoyed every second building that Video shop I felt like a pioneer a trailblazer for a while at least.

And at the end of it, all my mate Everett once asked: "here Jonny how come you have all this money"? I replied "because Spar man pays me well Everett" "can you get me a job as well then"? he asked me well it so happens once we had finished it needed publicizing and not having the luxury of social media back then Michael asked me one day if I knew anyone who would like to post leaflets all over from Darnley to Flanshaw to Peacock to Alverthorpe.

And one Sunday morning Everett turned up crack of the sparrows fart early morning start Michael came in his jag opened the boot this time with a big fat cigar in corner of his mouth a proper Del boy moment, "here you go kids get rid of all these for me "he said with excited enthusiasm in

99

his voice, and that's what we did we set about delivering thousands of leaflets Everett was well chuffed he had dropped on the money way I had "can't wait to get paid can you Jonny"? "nope I can't Everett "I says in a giddy tone of voice, we set about the task with real gusto and enthusiasm walked miles that day all over shop we did, legs aching and tired by time we had finished we arrived back on Flanshaw and met Michael back at the new Video shop

Tony was a hard worker even back then and we stood there excitedly waiting to be paid bundles Michael stares says "well-done kid's well-done thanks so much you're a good lad you Jonny and so is your mate here what's your name again youngen "? he asks Everett "Tony" replies Everett. " oh very good very good " Michael replies with that fat cigar hanging out corner of his mouth " he then digs his hand into his pocket and pulls out his fat wallet , full of the readies crispy green ones blue ones and brown he says "thanks a lot lads for helping out today and thanks once again Jonny for making the dream happen" I smiled and said "no problem Michael and thanks for Cigs an all " "No worries Jonny No worries" and then he says "go on then put your hands out kids" Everett all excited at this point looks at me smiling and began to slather at the mouth in anticipation ,we put our hands out and watched as he flicked the notes through his nicotine-stained but heavy tanned fingers with gold rings on each one and then it happened he goes and places in our hands a green one apiece ,

I'll never forget the look on Everett's face as we stared gone out at our hands looking up then looking down then looking up again in embarrassing astonishment at how much Michael had decided we were worth for our backbreaking efforts, yes a big fat green pound note came to rest softly in the palms of our hard-working beat to the bone hands, not the blue ones I had been getting whilst building the Video shop ,but green ones, So funny was Everett in his response first he looked at me then he looked at Michael and then back to me and then back to Michael and said thanks in a reluctant God I hate you kind of expression with a forced smile and when Michael turned around and said " no problem young man no problem at all and how would you like to do some more for me next week too"? Everett's face changed at the very thought and he looked at me and said: "yeah we can do can't we Jonny"?

And as we walked away Everett says leans over me cos he was much taller than me and says "I thought he paid you a fiver Jonny you lying sod "He did Tony he did "! I replied laughing not a care in the world personally as I still had a ton from the months of toil previously., So funny Was Everett when something wound him up and he replies "well I'll tell you this for nowt he won't get another minute of my time the tight twat a Poxy pissing Quid the tight fucker "at this point I was laughing uncontrollably so much my belly began to hurt. So, I say "Here why don't we go buy an elephants foot and chill out Tony sod it eh?"? "you fucking what? not a chance am I giving him his poxy Quid back for a poxy Elephants foot Jonny, not a frikkin chance the tight get I'll not do this again and here I, I say this for nowt an all he can go deliver his poxy leaflets himself next week an all! "

So that was that then, I still went and did my bit and delivered more leaflets for him as I felt a sense of loyalty to Michael and besides I did not share Everett's opinions he was always good to me anyway.

Chapter Eleven

The Silly Willy Affair

Summer was in full swing now me Jonna Our Mick John Ogdon Julie a lass called Violet an Irish girl who had moved into the tin houses all begun to converge on the Flanshaw Junior and infants school field we would sit on that field with not a care in the world and not up to anything as such just hanging about I had a habit back then of pulling the grass up around me where I lay and making a pile of it next to me on the ground, Why ? no idea it's sort of thing I did when I was bored pretty much like in the 70s when I would sit on the pavement scratching the moss out of the cracks in the pavement sort of thing it was just something to do with our hands until we thought of a new plan or something to do for the day, anyway when suddenly out of nowhere pops up Silly willy remember him? our resident tramp from years ago who had been chased by that bull down our street Well he turned up out of nowhere one day and as we were all a bit bored at the time we collectively allowed him into our fold mostly to relieve our boredom more than anything and so this particular day he was walking past bottom of the hill and I shout over "Willy how you doing "? Not seen you in ages and so he came over plonked his bike on grass and began smiling away and began chatting away with us, I never thought willy spoke much to be fair but by jolly could he speak for England, talked about all sorts mostly how he wanted to crack this person or that person who had done him wrong Willy was pretty much the butt end of many of the estates kids as he was a tramp and stuck out from the crowd a perfect target if you like?

anyway Violet one day turned up with a friend of hers called Julie a nice lass long dark curly hair quite shy but always had a smile but was for whatever reason a bit unsure of herself now we all knew she had not had a boyfriend before and we also knew Willy had not had a girlfriend either so we hatched a crazy plan to do a matchmaking, so I one day asked Willy " why don't you go into town get a haircut a shave and buy some new clothes because I reckon if you did you might pull that lass Julie Willy. Wouldn't you like a girlfriend? Willy just looked at me and began to laugh uncontrollably stood there in his wellies and donkey jacket in the near eighty odd degrees heat wiped a bit of sweat off his brow and replies "no Jonny no no no not a chance not a chance Jonny I like how I look and I won't change for no one especially some bloody female " he followed this up with uncontrollable laughter which had us all in stitches , so anyway after a few hours of us all frustratingly trying to convince him that if he did as he was told he might pull Julie, so one day Violet invited her up with us on the grass to laze away we had by now moved from the school field after I had grazed it with my bare hands so instead we climbed onto the old electrical hut just below it was a hell of a thing to climb as we were all so short so we improvised and would stack bricks up against its wall and climb up that way then once conquered lay in the sun on its warm surface for most part of the day and tell jokes stories about all sorts from football to music to women to what CB we owned all sorts or anything we would chat about atop of it, small talk winding away the summer holidays

so, one-day Willy turns up still dressed in his tramp attire donkey jacket with a rope wrapped around it god knows why he did that for? and his old brown nylon trousers tucked into his old tatty wellies riding his battered old push iron made up of all sorts of various bikes from gardens in and around the estate he tidied up for money,

So anyway, we all continued to ask him to beg him even until he finally broke so he pulls out this wad of cash and asked us laughing his head off hardly believing himself what he was about to do and his broad Yorkshire accent says "go on then how much do I need then eh "? Spoke with a wry grin on his face, Silly Willy you see was a tramp a fully-fledged tramp king tramp of the tramp world

but he knew how to make money he was loaded and rumour had it he would hide it down his wellies up his chimney under his bed the floorboards in his void of furniture house on Moorhouse Darnley he would hide it anywhere really apart from a bank,

 so anyway we said our goodbyes and he rode uptown and we all sat there giggling amongst ourselves wondering what he would look like all clean and tidy and later that day as the sun was coming down a figure appeared over the horizon and riding toward our direction, imagine music from magnificent seven as you picture it and you'll get my drift and as it got closer its face began to glimmer in the fading sun Silly Willy dressed in a brown pinstripe suit shiny new leather shoes a white shirt a brown tie the works a cleanly shaved riding that old mongrel push iron

 Smelling of Brut absolute gobsmacked we were and after many shouts of approval from us lot and me personally laid on field chewing a blade of grass I looked up and just remember seeing his tired old face smiling at us all never saw Willy smile much but my word was he soaking up the praise and his ego and self-worth finally given that boost it needed we just sat there on grass absolutely gobsmacked mostly because he no longer

looked the same bloke, no longer the loveable old tramp we came to love ,
Nope Willy was now a fully-fledged Gentleman and for some odd reason
he acted it too, it's hard to put into words and on paper how much
different he looked, anyway so once the excitement had settled and we
had finished filling up his head with some much-needed ego

we arranged to meet with him that night on the Electrical hut bottom of
flanshaw junior and infants school overlooking tin houses, and it actually
went very well Julie also was in on the plan and came dressed in a yellow
Rar Rar skirt white cotton coat some of those 80s dolly shoes white socks
with the frilly bits, you know the ones because us lads always called them
virgin socks whenever we saw a lass wearing them,

so this was turning into a bit of a love story we all jumped off the hut and
onto the school playing field drinking tins of pop eating from white paper
bags filled with a quarter of kops some ate sweet peanuts bought from
Frank Perry's earlier that day and generally had a great time and then
Corner of my eye I sees Willy and Julie snogging we all took a deep breath
and began to clap she just stopped us in our tracks and said shut it,
nutters,,,,,,, and we did and we all conveyed to them how chuffed we were
they were an item So Anyway that was that Fanshawe's very own love
story never mind that good looking, Ryan, o Neil we had Silly Willy no
contest
!

it was truly amazing to see two lonely people who needed some love and
ego building getting together like that and in that way , and it lasted too
well it did for about 6 months I think before Willy decided to fall back
naturally may I say back into his old ways and they parted ways but for a
moment in time we realized anything was possible if you pay it enough
attention people need a helping hand sometimes and that was pretty
much it as I remember it , and as the sun faded the leaves began to fall
and Xmas came and went my toy pile was becoming non-existent now
and socks and smellies took their place 1983 was now upon us and I
began to realize in 5 months' time I would be leaving high school and into
the big wide world of work

School was going ok not much happening apart from the skiving became more frequent now as May was approaching fast going to school did not seem as important anymore and that was a belief shared by my from teacher Mr Leigh he was a nice teacher he was different to the others a laid-back attitude and basically gave me the impression as an all-around nice guy and that as much as the school system had tried to educate us to put us on the right path to a rewarding career it was never going to be for me and counting the days down we sort of drifted from lesson to lesson awaiting the big day we seemed to be the outcasts the forgotten ones the ones that had been given a chance had failed miserably to take it so we ended up with Mr Leigh for those last few months

At morning register our class being so few we didn't even sit at our desks rather we would sit on the side of the classroom on the worktops where the gas taps were, causing a fuss amongst ourselves there was 8 of us in total in that final term in our class and 9 including Mr. Leigh he would welcome us in the morning shout our names for register and send us on our way not much was ever said apart from he would wish us all a good day and encouraged us half-heartedly to make most of the few lessons we had left , So there we were wondering the corridors like lost boys, like outcasts the system had given up on and we lived up to it the expectations everything often me and paddy would skip lessons and sit around the smokers corner and then it happened may was upon us May 28th to be precise and exams were for us nonexistent we never made it that far and we said our goodbyes to all the staff and our mates on that final day

I remember walking up the drive and onto Warmfield view and as I reached the top I looking over my shoulder and thinking to myself well that's that then, thinking no more getting up early anymore no more waiting at top of Flanshaw hill for 114 no more running downhill to GK Halls for 20 fags ,that final day at school was a bit of an anticlimax really never thinking that in years to come the world I had lived in since the age of 5 was such a small piece of the jigsaw of life and never thinking for one moment all the friends I had grown up with would all drift away in time and the new world I was about to grow into a man in awaited me, in the coming months after leaving school aged fifteen I spent a lot of my time over road at Joanne's listening to my old hero from 70s David Bowie and remembering reminiscing to her the old days with my mate Tigger in his bedroom when I had first heard him in his bedroom good times we also had a bit of a fling but nothing serious or owt.

CB was pretty much on its knees too now as British telecom made it illegal to own a am radio and introduced a license , whenever you introduce a license to anything that means rules and rules are meant to be broken as they say but it made no difference CB was on its knees and dying a slow death, but hey this was the 80s the decade of the entrepreneur was among us and attention now turned to the new fad of video nasties as they were called Watching videos with lots of blood and guts and gore was the new thing no longer Dracula or Frankenstein on our tellies on a Saturday night they soon vanished as the video age swept into our living rooms mum got one off slot telly man as a complete package we finally got our first colour tv and a matching video recorder in corner of our living room

I remember the excitement of rigging it all up for mum with our mick and switching it on for first time only catch was unlike folk who could afford one outright we had to pop a quid in a slot at back of the telly to watch anything and seeing my first video appear on our telly was incredible the sense of freedom you felt is hard to explain but if you were there as I was you will get my drift and that an all walking round to the video shop I helped build previously it's hard to explain how exciting it was renting films back in the 80s when it all began you have to remember that before this we only had the ABC minors in town which me and out Mick used to go to every Saturday morning to watch cartoons, but the freedom you felt renting videos on Saturday nights mostly was awesome always something new being released the market was flooded with all sorts to watch most horror films which were absolutely scary as hell used to watch all sorts Friday the 13th was my first horror movie absolutely scared my pants off, and porkies was my first comedy all about high school students getting up to no good with the girls etc. reminded me so much of my school days ,

what else did I get up to after leaving school? helped mum around the house and despite the video recorder we had sat in the corner of our living room that summer of 83 I spent mostly on the electric hut at Flanshaw first school with my old mates Wayne Oggy Jonna Violet our Mick and of course Big Godis even Silly Willy was still on the scene back to his old ways and dressed in his old tramp attire and not a care in the world being single once more after losing Julie the girl we had set him up with the months previous meant nothing to him Single life suited Willy, our attempts at domesticating him fell on death ears, suppose it was like taming a wild animal not a chance

So the world of work awaited me and my first job was a government scheme called YTS training for life most kids that had just left school ended up on one of these unless you were really educated of course which I was not so I ended up on Thatcher's Government scheme looking back on it all now and remembering looking forward to my first pay packet £25 a week I was getting I shall never forget my first day either we all were told to meet on chantry bridge by the toilets that used to be there stood in the freezing autumn air having what I never realized at the time my last summer and my last days of freedom though I never thought of this at the time anyway I bumped into a few old friends from school Bozer Andy jones mark Hibbert Paddy Naylor it felt weird seeing them dressed out of school uniform and we all stood there smoking our heads off talking amongst ourselves what might await us so we get through the doors and climbed some old stairs into what looked like old classrooms we sat there and was told what we were to do I was chosen to do paint and decorating along with my old mate Mark Hibbert

before our first job though we had a visit from the staff of a local TSB bank to explain to us how to look after our bank accounts that had been set up for us just remember these 2 attractive ladies explaining to us about how to use a chequebook what to write on it etc. how to deposit money and pretty much the a to z of saving kind of thing but I was never that good at saving because even back in the 70s I was earning some good money always blew it and when mum gave us that game to play with the catalogue and asking us to build a home with pretend money I never bought furniture like my siblings I was too interested in toys and having a good time , so the world of work although I enjoyed it I never really got ahead in it I always spent more than I earned and basically skint from week to week after paying my mum board and lodgings of £10 a week and buying my cigs I was skint every week my dreams of being rich were fading as was my ambitions

My first job was bottom of Westgate me and hobbit and boxer were all on the same team and our first job was decorating an old church on lawfield lane the smells of paint in the air as you walked through its doors on cold crispy mornings I'll never forget and our supervisor Charlie he was a right laugh treat us as one of the boys always telling crude jokes it felt weird being accepted as a young adult it was nice to be spoke to and not down to as we had at school and I really enjoyed being a decorator it was something I pursued later in life but for now the reality of it was I was on Thatcher's Youth training scheme so a day at work consisted of getting the paint kettles filled sandpaper and a rag in our overalls and we set about for the first few weeks never even touching a   paintbrush we just sanded and sanded the hell out the walls and not small ones either this was a massive church hall and we had to assemble scaffolding scary to climb bit once on top we were fine we did all that church hall and as the weeks rolled on I really enjoyed the work I was putting into refurbishing this old church hall

I began to take a pride in what I was doing and looked forward to my pay packet at end of the week , But like anything it was never meant to last I was to keen to earn more money without thinking the benefits of a good apprenticeship would bring me I decided to leave and get a job in the mill where our Norm worked the third oldest of my siblings he had worked there from time began and asked me if I would like a job there our Mick was working there and I remember coming home although satisfied and happy at decorating he had more money than me forty five quid a week to be exact so when our Norm asked me if I would like a job there as a place had opened up I eagerly said yes and departed with a heavy heart from decorating and went to work finally into a full-time job at a textile Mill Rawson's on Portobello estate , I took it because although in the long term Decorating was a trade and once completed I would go on to earn some really good money but I was young and dumb back then and wanted riches now not in years to come

so I took up our Norms offer and met the personnel officer at Rawson's a dark old satanic mill it was I remember walking through its doors and into a posh office nothing like the filthy dusty factory that awaited me so Roy forgot his second name now but anyway he sat me down and I'm there all nervous not knowing if I was going to make a good impression or not but soon realized I did not have to try that hard he asked me if Norman was my brother I said yes and that was about it really he offered me the job there and then the interview lasted all of 5 minutes ! he then told me how much I would earn forty-five pound a week which was twenty more than the YTS wow I thought that's easy money and after a handshake to that sealed my first full-time job I walked out that door head held high I couldn't wait for Monday to come and it did come very quickly I woke up made my way downstairs at absolutely silly o clock in the morning so early, in fact, it was still dark outside! never been up this early before was my thoughts at the time so I sit on our settee eating toast and drinking tea with our Norm and Mick even had telly on an all very unusual for such an early morning as this, a new morning show had started called tv am just remember sat there in amazement with my brothers watching posh folk that Anne Diamond on telly up at same time as us yawning same as we did tired same as we were I felt a connection and thinking maybe these posh folk on telly are no different to us and for years after this first early morning experience the theme tune became my wakeup call my alarm if you like?

   Mum and my sister were still in bed, and we sat discussing blearily eyed, mouths over our tea cups holding them with two hands wrapped round it to stay warm cos coal fire was never made at this time only got made when mum got up, so he's telling me what to expect when we got there our Norm saying to me anxiously " and don't let me down youngen just do as you told" and with that we made our way to bottom of Flanshaw hill trudging through that crispy snow that had hardened overnight and in our steal toe cappers donkey jackets and beany hats to keep the wind off our ears we made our way to the bus shelter bottom of Flanshaw hill freezing cold morning still dark and eerily quiet I had never seen flanshaw so early like this before only when we used to go midnight mooching as kids but never in the winter besides we were always at school, strangers in the bus shelter most likely my mates mums and dads I'd never seen before also waiting to start the weekly grind all looking miserable as hell, there was Mr. Charlesworth my first friend on Keswick Michael Charlesworth's dad *he stood alongside us with his work satchel over his shoulder and wearing his Railway issue Donkey jacket, always smiling not like rest of grumpy sods stood there with us he was obviously used to this early morning thing same as our Norm was, they both had been working years before while I played out and went to school, so he turns to me and says jokingly "Welcome to real world Jonny Boy not in your bubble anymore now tha knows" said in a jokingly manner , then asks "how's your mam these days ? oh nearly forgot Cath has told me to tell you to send her over at 7 pm tonight for a coffee and a Cal "*

Cath and me Mum was proper to chitter chatters, what they didn't know about folk on Keswick Drive wasn't worth knowing about, always said things tongue in cheek did Mr Charlesworth he nicknamed me mum Maggie T after prime minister cos her hair used to look exactly same as hers, I wasn't too keen on that name or my mum having that hairstyle but I'm an old punk so I went with flow really,

so, I replies "she's fine Mr Charlesworth" "" and in mid-sentence he stops me in my tracks, "Call me Mick from now on Jonny" and there suddenly at that moment I felt like a man a proper bloke one of the lads etc. my first taste of the real world happened there and then. Anyway, me our Mick Our Norm and Mick Charlesworth stood there making small talk in freezing cold a nice bloke was Mick though his Wife Cath used to send me to shop for cigs and Lucozade in the 70s and he also had built me my first proper bicycle a ten-speed green metallic racer one Christmas I still say hello to him to this day and his daughter Lisa also still a good friend of mine so anyway, where was I? oh aye so it was weird standing at that old bus shelter but it was nothing like the happy go lucky gang we had whilst waiting for that 114-school bus only months previous top of hill. And then a bus appears coming down one way from the hotel I asked our Norm Nervously "is that our bus then?" he said no it was the double two shirts work bus I remember it used to pull up and loads of women would gawp out its windows what felt like at the time dead embarrassing for a sixteen-year-old lad, to be honest so I adjusted my tact and I soon learned to stand back in the shadows whenever it pulled up, in the meantime our bus finally arrived we pulled up over road from lumps ices and walked the short walk to the main gates I remember that walk felt like an eternity all I wanted to

Chapter Twelve

Time for A Job

met me at the main gates and walked me down this long dark dusty corridor smells of grease and oil wafted through the air and the dust from the old wooden beams above my head fell onto my face as I walked the long walk to this big machine I was about to learn about and get started on,

So anyway he gets to end of this corridor my brothers waved me bye and shouted over noisy machines that they would see me in canteen at break time, it was then I suddenly realized I wouldn't be working with them the disappointment was real the sense of anguish unbearable, here I was a 16year-old kid first day at work realizing I was to be working on my own ,and as I nervously followed Roy up that small flight of crumbling old stairs and into this dimly lit old room I was greeted with the sight of piles and piles, rows upon rows stacked easy 20 high of old single mattresses, I looked at them, I looked at Roy, he looked at me, I looked at him, we sort of repeated this a few times until it became all rather awkward and I just stood there wondering what the hell I was to do with that lot ?, and then Roy opens his mouth and begins his sermon "here you go, young man this is a Stanley knife I want you to cut open these mattresses and take out all the cotton put it on this trolley and push it over to number 8 machine in the Garnet he then proceeded to give me a demonstration made it look easy an all and I thought well maybe this isn't so bad after all, but it meant working on my own no mates to pass the daily grind away with .

Thoughts of high school came back to me I was missing school a lot no one told me working life was going to be like this though, the Garnet department, by the way, was where I thought I was going to be working ,it was a massive room with really old rugged textile machinery clunking banging and grinding away the noise was repetitive dusty as hell and deafening it smelled of glue and old rags that second-hand shop smell the machines stood side by side and had a few men on each , but I wanted a piece of that working on them usually meant folding fillings for mattresses they rolled of a wooden latté conveyor etc. it was menial mundane job but kept you on your toes but still in my mind it beat cutting up mattresses. I guess this was my test, my initiation if you like? Suppose looking back on it to test if I cut the mustard or not, whether I was up to the job well course I was I was from Flanshaw wasn't I? So I got stuck in the minutes turned to hours the hours turned to days the days turned to weeks and so on and as the second week started I now had developed blisters on the palms of my soft teenage hands but being a determined young bugger I worked through the pain and as crap as it was I became quite close to this job as the months went by I realized that working in other parts of the mill meant being watched over by a boss , at least in here I was my own boss and so on early mornings I would even sneak on top of the piles of mattresses and right to back and get my head down for an hour while rest of the mill worked so it had its perks, I would cut right into the pile and bring it right down only to be met with a thousand more the following day it was like taking two steps forward and four back and I realized I was never going to get rid of them all so, a few months later I gets a visit from Roy "how's it going young man? "he asked "its ok mate "I replied and he says to me "follow me" so I did and he led me to number 8 machine in garnet "this machine needs a new helper John and you fit the bill do you want it?" do I want it? I thought of course I did and I gladly accepted I threw away that old Stanley knife and acquainted myself with the lads One was called Joe a West Indian lad off Portobello then there was Wilf a small stocky bloke with curly hair who welcomed me on board as he was the chargehand and then there was Ali one big family and that was it part of the gang finally I had made it into the promised land of milk and honey or in my case of human contact and a bonus on top of my wage!

"So, your Norms young Brother then"? Wilf the Boss asked me with a grin, he always had a grin did Wilf one of those grins that said I'm hiding something from you kind of grin I reply "yeah for my sins I suppose " to *rounds of laughter as they all heard me "so you're a grafter then are you? we only have grafters on this machine lad" said Wilf "aye, of course, I am you should know to see as I've supplied your machine with cotton for the past 3 months " Wilf replies "aye but that was easy part this is where we sort men out from boys you know ?" I'd heard this banter before and I looked him in the eye and said " here I'm from Flanshaw me and that's all you need to know mate" Wilf replies "alright lad then let's get you started shove in those cotton bails toward Hopper for Joe a Hopper was basically a machine that tore the cotton up into small manageable pieces to go through the machines combs etc. and even though it was back breaking I got my head down and did as I was told never tried to be too clever or owt I just got on with it and it worked*

As I soon became one of the team on number 8 as Wilf said so after a few weeks ! what a moment that felt for a 16-year-old kid I'll never forget that feeling of pride it ran through my veins and gave me a real buzz ,I suddenly felt like a man in a man's world and it was great ! and soon I found myself being used as a utility man whenever someone was absent I would fill their place and this was great as It meant I got an average bonus off each machine some weeks I took home as much as seventy pounds a week . It wasn't as easy as old days running to shop for folk on my Keswick drive or building a Video Shop but this was the real world and as crap as the work was the lads I worked with were fantastic and over the years there we became like family, there were, however, jobs I hated too like the chopper in washer department basically back breaking work like you wouldn't believe it involved bending over all day picking up old rags off a pile and feeding them into a guillotine type of thing that chopped the fabric up into small pieces which then became fillings for mattresses etc. hated that job and whenever old Tommy the boss in there came mooching into the garnet for someone to run it I would sneak off for a fag in the toilets and out of his way before he had chance to collar me this was an advantage on number 8 machine as it was right next to his department and besides Wilf When he could get away with it would cover for me as he wanted me on his machine I did not escape it every time but most times I did

And this brings me onto my first proper mate at work weird bloke not very tall brown curly hair always wore an army jacket and glasses he was blind in one eye and he spoke with a bit of a high pitched voice but not feminine if that makes sense? anyway, a bit of a loner loved a good rant about management and always happy but he had this ritual he used to walk in Canteen always sat at the end of our table and at break times the noise of folk chatting and the usual banter and ongoing conversations would always fall silent whenever he walked in. Bit like a spaghetti western scenario when unwanted cowboys would walk in a bar for a whiskey or three, anyway so this was his ritual so read on , unzip satchel bring out glass cup open Thermos flask pour Tea into glass cup 2 tablespoons sugar into glass cup stir glass cup (loudly as he could) and not just stir he spun that bloody tea bag as loud as the twin tub of me mams spun me clothes , and this rather odd ritual would go on for about 3 minutes he would then reveal a Kit Kat chocolate bar snap one of its pieces in two and insert both pieces in his mouth at the same time then lift his cup of tea and wash down the said

Kit Kat in one,

He would then look up, me and the lads would stop our game of cards we just sat their silent jaws dropped "hi guys how are you all today ? " to which Hunty our stacker driver would always have a friendly insult "aye were fine Bamber was just a bit concerned about you lad does thee after stir thi tea like that "?

he would snigger back and know damn well what we were getting at but he got the attention and he milked it every time, personally I liked him where the older blokes would say to me "you want to stay away from that weirdo" but I liked a rebel I like anyone who bucked the trend the normal the conformity and the Late Raymond Birkby AKA Bamber RIP ticked all my boxes we hit it off pretty much instantly he loved all the latest technology the latest gadgets of the time VHS players latest HIFI separates cd players and so on he was a geek was Ray but I loved all that had some right parties at his flat on Linton road with his homemade specialities I became a bit of a utility Boy/ man for a while and whenever I was moved to the Jute shredding department I knew it was going to be an easy day because I knew Bamber never maintained machines properly and every so often the machine would break down usually a bit of Jute stuck in the ducting pipes that were attached to the machine nowt to stress over cos it could be easily fixed with no need to call for a fitter I would have to shout over cos the machines in there were noisy as buggery hell "it's blocked again Bamber" the machine was on his Blind side cos of his glass eye and Ray being Ray and being a tad eccentric he would run up to the machine in an aggressive manner which I thought was funny and with a flying Hong Kong fuey kick smash the safety guard rail unfortunately for him he would miss the intended target and land on his arse ! And I knew at this point I would get a quick smoke break because he always stood up took a deep breath brush himself down and say "Sod it lets go grab a fag, Jonny" "sod it aye Bamber " I would say back to him with sly a grin on my face it was easy to skive off work with Ray all you had to do was get him chatting about the latest gadgets VHS players and cd players and an hour or two later he would say "well we best get some work done " Rawson's was a dusty horrible place to work in conditions were terrible but the lads were second to none

I remember the Christmas times there we would all eagerly talk over canteen table or a game of Darts on the knackered old cork dartboard on wall what bonus we might get having a bit of banter with one another who would earn most which machine was king blah blah blah we also got double money at Xmas too which helped not that it did me cos I would blow most of it on five cards turn over, a card game we played religiously at break times I was crap at it but a tad addicted and also the works raffle never won sod all but that sticks in my mind and then the nights out in Wakefield on final day of work always remember bat out of hell playing on jukebox in wine lodge first time I got drunk drinking with proper blokes I was on my arse after five pints Christ I was only sixteen years old being carried to the Strafford by me mate Hunty the stacker driver then waking up next morning with me Mam shouting down me lughole "get up" happy times

So towards the end of 1983 and having survived my first Xmas night out with proper blokes life was looking good bit of money in the bank not a lot but enough to not be skint from week to week I remember that year my eldest Brother Steve he bought one of those new 2 stroke motorcycles Suzuki X7 and he rode it over to our house one day, loved motorbikes when I was a kid me and Tigger used to play on his old field bike over grazzy remember ? so I rushes out of our garden gate posts to have a look a beauty she was red metallic paintwork with chrome all over shop, I begged our Steve for a spin on it but somehow knew the answer would be no and deep down It was too powerful anyway turns out it was the first 2 stroke Japanese bike to hit one hundred miles per hour, Well that's what our kid said so I says to him "take us for a spin then?" " that's what I was going to suggest" says our Steve and with that he unclipped the spare Lid *from under the seat "put this on then" and he fastened it tight for me, me mum came out to have a look too "Just taking our Jonny for a spin mum" said our Steve and all she could say was "well just go careful pair on yh" and with that he kicks it over and we set off slow pace along Keswick towards Grazzy field turned right and headed for Batley road once on there we still went at snail's pace and I'm sat on back thinking well this is a bit crap Tiggers 50 field bike went faster than this so we gets past Crown pub on the left our Steve looks over his shoulder at me and gives me the ok sign then suddenly we were off like a rocket I held onto his jacket for dear life we banks to right headed towards Star pub over motorway bridge past the water tower down a country lane and we turned around at babes in the wood crossroads last time I had made this journey was when I used to go to the Sidings and to see me old bird Christine never forgot her or the happy times we had there . 1984 was creeping along and folk used to talk about this because it was the year George Orwell predicted the world would change Bowie sang a song about it ! how right he was looking back on it all, this was beginnings of the digital age VCR recorders High fi separates Compact disc players Video games machines even a home computers were out in the shops even mobile phones if you had the money to buy one although they were size of a brick but these times I lived in were the beginnings of the digital age what we see today it did not dominate our lives as it did back then though as there was no internet just yet, but personally looking back on it all it was always going to improve and it was only a matter of time before the world wide web was amongst us. So it came nothing noticeable happened to us as that clock struck twelve on new year's eve 1983 I went back to work as did many others and we moved on with our lives 1984 was well and truly among us I was now the shop lad in the Garnet and I enjoyed that as it meant I got a bigger share of everyone's machines bonus I filled in on the machines when someone was Ill off work and this would carry on up into the summer where finally I got to work on Garnet number 3 machine much cushier than the other machines as it made big rolls of underlay me and Gilly me mate who ran it at the time would spend hours while the roll at end of machine got bigger we could spend a good hour sat on our arses waiting for it to reach the length the order book said and in those moments we would chat about all sorts mostly the Foreman Bill and his assistant Mick they were both a bit eccentric Bill for instance always used to get angry if a machine broke down unlike Ray in Jute who would kick the bloody thing thinking that would get it working again Bill was more audible in his frustrations although I often witnessed the odd hammer or spanner fly past my head when things went arse up he got angrier than owt so when our machine would break down me or Gilly the chargehand at the time would shout him over if we could not mend it with tools we had at our disposal "what's happened " ? Mick would say with a concerned look on his face as though he had just lost a member of his family "machines broke down mick" I would say with a don't give a toss look on my face "well how come"? what a silly question and what a silly man I thought "well I'll have a look at it then"*

and he would and me and Gilly would humour him say how good he was and how knowledgeable he was we did this so we could sneak off for a fag in toilets and it worked every time cos he would turn round and say well leave it to me lads, So let me describe the fag area at Rawson's the toilets it was a doorway the entrance as you walked in was a pile of coconut hair fibre mats on the floor that was seconds out of the fibre department and this is where I met all the characters always some banter going off in here and remarks that today you would be locked up for but back in the day black brown or white we all gave as good as we got and there was always respect among us then there was Tony he thought he was right hard him he would walk in toilets and shove his weight around no one actually liked him that much cos he seemed to be a bit personal in his insults Black joe used to cop it most but Joe being joe always took it on the chin to Tony's dismay then there was Viv a good looking son of a Miner from Hemsworth looked like George Michael and boy did he want everyone to know an all, He was a right poser was Viv, he worked with our norm on 8 and 8 machines they hated each other but worked well in order to get the biggest bonus in Garnet and although most

didn't like Viv once again I did as he was a bit of an outcast he was funny as hell every payday just before being paid he would walk in the bogs on a smoke break and ask "how much bonus do you think you will get today John"? I would always say not enough mate to which he would always Reply"well I'm going to get nearly as much as your wage in bonus and that means I'll only have £180 left after that to last me a week his eyes rolling at this point,! how the hell will I survive eh"? annoying? yes but also funny and as I was trying to get away politely he then chirps up with "on top of that I have the most beautiful woman in the world I met last week in town she and all her friends wanted me and all" .he was always Bragging off was Viv but I took him with a pinch of salt but turns out Gilly once told me the bird he met that night in Wakey had slept with his mate on an old mattress over Bella much for the Stud status eh? Poor Viv he lived in a bit of a fantasy world but he was really funny to those who understood his humour though as I did, he once came in bogs sat next to me and said "Hey John I'm not bragging or owt" he always started his sentence with this "well I'm not bragging or owt john but I was in town last night and I had eight women who wanted my body do you think its out to do with cos I look like George Michael? and my stubble chin"? I always cracked up when he got off on one funny bloke was Viv, and that's a little journey into some of my mates I worked with

Chapter Thirteen

A Bike Is Needed

So, in the summer of 1984 I was getting itchy feet I wanted a motorbike I sent for my provisional in the meantime I would go on back of our Norm on his Yamaha DT 100 he bought at the time little trial bike with a red blue and white tank I was desperate for a bike I hated riding pillion it scared me and our kids riding skills were not so great so I thought I either buy my own or I will be dead before I get a chance to. And so, I did few months into the summer just after my seventeenth birthday I bought our kids DT 100 he had bought the X7 off our Steve and I naturally bought his and so there we were a bike apiece parked in our backyard

Owning me own bike was an awesome feeling freedom to come and go as I chose the world was suddenly a smaller place suddenly I had that independence bug I would ride up and down the s bends on Flanshaw road at silly speeds and how I never piled it up on their I'll never know thing is I was and still can be a bit of a loose cannon I just seem to do before I think now 50 years old I realize that life is a game of averages and sooner or later you're going to come to a cropper and I did one rainy night heading down Balne lane to Bamber's flat on Eastmoor I took the right-hand bend at the junction of Silcoates on Peacock the one just before the former Library I wasn't really going that fast cos of the rain but I was addicted to banking it down and with it being such a light motorcycle I did exactly that no protective gear just my jeans and a belstaff jacket I had found in the rags at Rawson's and over I went the Bike slipped from underneath me and I skidded all the way up to the chippy about 20 yards on my bare knees it was the shock of it all it never hurt at the time it happened but I do remember seeing the surface bone of my knee cap and I recovered I survived this was a harsh lesson on how not to ride a bike, my bike was
not in bad nick, to be honest, lucky for me I had left the rear foot pegs down and that took most of the impact lucky for me it saved the paintwork, anyway so I rode up to the hospital and had my self-cleaned and strapped up etc. then went home and died for a few days never told my mum and kept my self-covered up cos she would have worried if she knew I had been an idiot so I explained my limp away by saying I had a

sprained ankle she believed me she always believed owt you said me, mum, she was too kind sometimes too polite for her own good.

And I guess growing up we had no boundaries after nan died that's not to me mum's detriment though, she did alright even though she was and still is a soft touch she commands respect from us all without ever asking for it if that makes sense? Whereas my Nan, I'm sure would have read the riot act to me she was so loving but hard on us too firm but fair is the phrase I'm looking for here, so anyway, in a nutshell, I learned a harsh lesson and Luckily for me our Steve was a bike instructor up at that old building top of Balne lane on right as your climbing the hill I told him in confidence what had happened and surprisingly he handled my dilemma well not the response I expected so there I was a week later sat in a classroom with fellow wannabe bikers learning about road safety etc. there were many funny moments on this course such as one time we were doing a Night ride through town and we stop at traffic lights bottom of Westgate well this woman on her Honda 90 she did all the right things look over shoulder et before stopping break gently but that's where it ends cos not only did she break perfectly she also forgot to put her feet on the floor she toppled over like a skittle before our eyes that was nearly the strangest one I ever saw the one that topped this was a night rife through Winterset

The guy in Front was a lad called Kevin short skinny lad what a character he was, he wore jam jar glasses and wore one of those old half face helmets your grandad used to wear in the war he also wore a flying jacket and a long Scarfe basically looked like Biggles so anyway were riding along country lanes in a staggered formation as to not bump into the person in front of you in case we had to emergency stop and Kevin was leading the way he rode a good line too as we approached the first really bend he kept a good line only thing is he never strayed from this what appeared to be a perfect line and me riding behind him and I'm thinking "go on turn you, bloody idiot" ! But Kevin was a bit simple in the grey matter department and headed in a perfectly straight line into the hedgerows he flew over the hangers and landed in a farmers field it was like a scene from a keystone cop movie but having said after many a giggle and a lecture from our Steve on making sure to steer left when you hit a left bend we moved on and as time went by I grew in confidence I shook off my know it all head and got stuck into the theory and practical back on those days thought the only theory test was a few questions from a highway code book the majority was practical so I took my test on Leeds Rd. just past Vic Corner shined my bike up for the occasion and attacked it with confidence I passed the first time ! unbelievable I was over the moon and as I rode along Leeds Rd. back to Flanshaw as I approached the roundabout just before the old roundhouse at Newton Hill my number plate fell off ! wow lucky if this had happened on my test I would have instantly failed

Yes I certainly rode my luck that day excuse the pun felt great chucking my L plates away I took a detour under that old railway bridge that leads on to Peacock fields and I threw em away their and that was it my first proper Achievement as a 17-year-old kid first time I had ever gained any kind of reward for my efforts so it probably meant more to me than say the Brainy folk who did well at School so I get home and tells me, mam,, her first words were "well don't go getting a bigger bike just yet" she was always fearful of me having a Bike and now that I m a parent I can see how she must have felt cos there was three of us in family with motorbikes now me our Norm on X7 and our Steve who had bought himself a Honda CB 550 FII right beast was that in its day shiny red blue and white and went like a rocket we kept that from me, mam, though, so there I was 17 years old full bike license it was about this time I was knocking around on Darnley quite a lot with a mate I had met off CB years earlier Dave Brown he had a few Brothers Kev and Graham, I also got on right well with Graham an all so anyway Dave was only a little lad so he made perfect pillion passenger on my little DT 100 we started going up Eastmoor to me work mates Bamber's flat on Linton rd. he held some right Parties Did Ray his flat was really small with just a small living room and kitchen but he kept it right neat and tidy he was the homebrew and we spent many a night with sex pistols blasting out of his Sony separates he had bought out of the catalogue pogoing away I bumped into my old school pal Steve England an all cos he lived over road and he used to come round all-time with his sisters Karen and Tracey we all used to get smashed in the front room he even went to the lengths of buying some red blue green disco lights and had those flashing away an all it was a proper disco.

At about this time mid-1984 Arolds opened its doors to what remained of the CB radio users it was the last eyeball as I remember, punk really had helped me lose my inhibitions in those early days in the 70s

I remember used to go there every Friday night With Steve and his sisters, my brother Mick also came along as did Godis Bamber strangely never came anyway nelly the elephant used to get played here a lot and me and Steve would pogo as high as we could and headbutt the glittery disco ball spinning above our heads we got kicked out regularly for this god knows how we never got into fights we never intimidated anyone it was not the Punk way suppose we looked a bit intimidation although I had dropped the punk clothes years before we must have just been ugly god knows ? thing is punk had virtually disappeared now and only the gimmick bands like toy dolls got a look in and we milked it for as long as it lasted and admired the attention we got it was still fun being able to pogo about not a care in the world and all at the ripe old age of seventeen but the world was changing and also my family world too my sister moved out with her boyfriend towards the end of the year and that left me our Mick and Norm at home and away from my world which was changing and evolving things were changing out there in the big wide world too as this was the year our Miners went on strike I remember it well at work the debate raged on some did not support it some did the ones who did not support it was the ones who kept their head down never made waves with bosses the ones that never skipped work and nip off for a fag break like me and Gilly and me other mates did and the debates would always kick off while sitting in canteen someone would be reading the newspaper and another would make a comment about the front page which usually painted the miners in a bad light

I always supported the miners I didn't understand the struggle at the time I was too young and too naïve when it came to politics so I left it to the blokes to argue it out, I used to sit there my head going left to right, too and throw like you do when watching tennis on telly thinking wow were all working in this shit hole being paid a load of crap for the amount of work we put in and still men on both sides of fence some supporting Thatcher it was unreal, look I didn't understand it at all but those early days of punk back in 70s had taught me one thing, that anyone in authority is the enemy and Thatcher was the enemy she split the working class into two camps the ones on her side were the ones who bought their council houses and a few shares tell bloody Sid ads were running constantly on our telly buy shares here buy shares there anyway they had the exteriors plastered with god knows what it's called but it made their house look right posh and they all got a bit above themselves stopped talking to their neighbours the community I had grown up in was falling apart yes there were some on Keswick who thought they lived in a castle who previously been good neighbours but Thatcher changed all that it was as though she had cast a spell over good honest working folk, folk I had grown up with that's probably why they sang ding dong the witch is dead when she died. Anyway, to cut a long story short I listened to them all in canteen proud working blokes tearing into one another while that woman in number ten planned her war on working class anyway in end the Miners lost they had not a prayer the whole system seemed to turn on them and they went back to work following year heads held high. The media milked it patronized them called them sensible for giving up the same media who months previous had attacked them so venomously

I realized that year the world I was living in was not the same world I was brought up in and those innocent childhood days on Keswick Drive I had the privilege to have enjoyed and the great community spirit I was brought up in was now on its knees. Anyway enough of that this book is about my childhood experiences and that was certainly one of them but if you want to know more about what that woman did to our country there are plenty of books out there that will enlighten you, so back to my world the summer of 1984 still bombing around the estate on my DT 100 taking those s bends on flanshaw like a mad man I soon noticed a small gang had started to appear on the granny flats wall just before Flanshaw shops by the bridge over the beck I used to burn up and down the s bends showcasing my not so good bike skills taking bends at silly speeds they seemed to enjoy it either that or they thought I was a mental person god knows anyhow I pulled over one night me mate Browny was with me they were me old school friends from Saint micks Sharon and Tracey they were sisters and for some unknown reason I always got their names mixed up there was also Angela a bit younger than Sharon and Tracey she also had a younger sister called Paula also there was Michaela and her sister Jackie and also Michelle a blonde haired lass her boyfriend at the time was my old school mate Andy Williams then there was Lloyd who was going out with Julie I think her name was she went to Saint Micks but was right

quite she lived right on s bends in the corner house and then a lad called
Neil a larger than life character always cracking jokes and the clown of
the gang so we sits down sparks up a roll up and got chatting about bikes
in general what we would like to own what we wouldn't want to own etc.
etc. that kind of thing, they were all drinking Kestrel lager from VG at the
time the granny flats wall was the drinking wall the meeting place
everyone or anyone drank on this wall so the lads got up and looked my
bike over it was nowt special but it got their attention all the same, and
the term back then if you was a bit crazy was a mad hatter Neil was first
to call me that. "seen you bomb up and down here these her past few
weeks you're a mad hatter thee is John" laughing as he said this. I took
his words as a compliment I really did as if that was my initiation into
their fold and it went from there really, we would all meet up on the wall
after work some of them like Paula in her case after School

The world was changing fashion was too and I found my self-wearing
those stretch light denim jeans and a pair of slipper type shoes you could
buy from Jonathan James top of Westgate didn't need to lace them up
either , and the lasses wore hug boots and jeans usually had tie dye
patterns in them the lasses all seemed to wear sheepskin coats an all for
some odd reason Angela had a grey one the rest wore Brown , so there
you have it and that's what I found my self-doing dossing about on that
wall on Flanshaw it became our hang out and when I wanted to have a
drink which was very rare I liked riding my bike too much but occasionally
I would leave it parked in back garden at home and walk round but most
times those summer evenings were spent watching them all get drunk
then over time Andy Williams got himself a bike a Kawasaki AR 50 Then
Neil ended up with a Yamaha RD 50 another lad soon joined us on the
wall too a quite lad called Alan Mycoe he had a Suzuki GT 180 ram air nice
bike even if it was a tad old his brother Kev bought a Suzuki ER 50 and
pretty much soon we all ended up with Motorbikes it sort of evolved
without anyone really taking notice and before long the gang grew in
number a lad called Biffy he lived in tin houses he soon joined us too he
rode a Kawasaki AR 50 too I think and thing what always bugged me with
Biffy was he never fastened his frikkin helmet always telling the sod to
fasten up he just grinned and said "aye I know" well by now we all pretty
much had a Machine to play on. Boys toys heaven as they say

It's hard to describe the camaraderie we built with one another on that wall and the subject after talking about our mundane day at work always led on to Bikes you see Bikes were king nowt was better than a good chat about what we were going to do with our Machines how we wanted to custom paint them we talked about the latest Air filters the latest exhaust pipes, racing reeds, fork braces, the latest oversized racing compound tyres, about the bikes we would like how fast we had been on such and such a road how close we had come to falling off the mad mile I was the only one at the time who had passed my test so I was able to take those without a bike on back of me and soon my regular passenger became Angie used to take her down mad mile many times and without consciously aware of it we fell into a relationship soon after you see thing is about Angie she loved her soaps even back then she liked the comforts of sitting in front of the telly to catch up on such shows at the time as Dallas the Colby's Eldorado Emmerdale farm EastEnders was not around until a year later and we watched that together too in our front room on Keswick everyone had been talking about this show since it had been mentioned all over the news it promised to be a gritty in your face drama that would get right in your face with harsh realities of life and it delivered too it did exactly what it said on the tin Angie loved all that

Whereas I was more interested in riding my bike and spending my nights on the wall anyway I always gave in and would sit agonizingly through episodes of Dallas and the above mentioned so never got to play out with the lads until after 8 pm most nights but that was ok I suppose I could live with it, well because we were a bit in love I suppose me and Angie stuck together for a few years and it all ended in heartache but I'll get on to that bit later. In the meantime read on. So back to the present and so I was by now beginning to get itchy feet and I wanted a new bike all that talk on the wall with me mates motivated me I simply had to have a new one and temptation finally got the better of me when one night we were sat on the wall talking about the usual stuff when I saw a headlight top of the hill by the Flanshaw hotel obviously a bike the engine on it sounded absolute mint ! it approached at speed and the rider was a short stocky lad the bike in question pulled out of a steep bank from the s bends and shot off up the hill popping a wheelie as it did so. We all looked at each other in awe gobsmacked "what the hell was that"? I said to everyone , it *had a custom paint job fluorescent orange and white custom sprayed basically a replica of the Marlborough race bikes I saw on the telly Well to cut a long story short I was simply in awe of it it was a beautiful machine chromed up to the knackers it also had chrome ace bars over the front of the hangers and was basically an all-around beast and it was only a learner bike a Yamaha RD LC 125 its rider went out with one of the lasses on the wall Michaela one night he pulled up and sat with us all introduced himself etc. "I'm Daz," he said and we all got chatting about his bike how could we not though? it stuck out like a sore thumb compared to ours parked up on paving flags where we used to park them and He was a nice fella was Daz a tad eccentric and a bit loud at times some would say a bit full of himself but I loved all that I liked his attitude I loved an outsider remember? And I couldn't compliment his bike enough, so I'm thinking to myself I want an LC, in fact, I need an LC*

And as time went by we was now well into the autumn the bigger our gang grew the louder we became and there was an old bloke used to come out his flat with a stick and threaten us with it "get the f**ck out of here you little ba***rds this is for old people round here " he would say and to be honest looking back at it now we were cruel and a tad disrespectful and would goad him on a bit and shout things, like get back in you old so and so etc. until one day he came out with a knife and looked a bit angrier than he had ever done previously, I was by now beginning to feel a bit sorry for him and that wasn't just me but most the lasses expressed this too also the police started turning up and moving us along then one day a copper pulls up and I'm thinking I know him from somewhere well it turned out to be Mr Austwick the old math's teacher from Eastmoor High he gets out the car and comes over to us and says argghh holey and what you up to these days ? and answering his own question before I had chance to "not very much by look of it nothing changes does it, Holey" and he moved us on he was a strict bugger was old Austwick and he got his way that night an all " Well Holey if I find you or any of your mates on this wall after six o clock in future I'll arrest lot of you got it " ? and while he said this he was looking at me the whole time with his evil eyes, so in the end we moved along fearful of arrest and we found our new home at the top of Flanshaw hill there used to be a bench there for as long as Flanshaw had been built it must have been cos it was right old and tatty but we didn't mind and it became our new home our gathering place,

So by now autumn was approaching work was going ok and I was approached by Bill the Garnet foreman and asked if I would like to take charge of number three machine as Gilly my mate was moved onto another machine that paid better bonus if I remember correctly I could be wrong here but I think that's how it when it was a bit sad really because me and Gilly used to crack jokes all day about Bill and his assistant fitter Mick with really blue stuff that I cannot mention on these pages, unfortunately, all I will say is they were of a what-if scenario ? so life was good promotion my money went up and first reactions was RD LC even though I had passed my test a 125 was still the better option for insurance purposes it also gave me a chance to ride a more powerful machine for a fraction of the cost so I went along with it and rode all over shop trying to find a decent one for right money and then I had a random ride over to Featherston high street one day and there low and behold was my dream Bike unbelievably it was the same bike as Daz had and I just had to have it and I bought it there and then seven hundred and fifty quid finally a bike to be proud of it was the ultimate machine chrome Micron exhaust and a k
& n Air filter it and once all the paperwork had been sorted out I took our Norm over on my old DT he rode that home I rode the beast home

And the start of my love affair had begun it rode like a dream smooth as owt and also had a couple of powerbands one at 5600 rpm and another kicked in at around 10.000 rpm top end I did 97 mph which may not sound much but considering my old DT only did 45 mph it was quite a step up so I get to top of Flanna Hill on it and everyone seemed as excited as me that I had it no one in the world not even myself would believe I would get same as Daz had but I did and rest is history and so the fun began racing Alan up and down Batley rd. that was one of the first requests everyone wanted to see a dual between my LC and the Suzuki GT 185 of Alans and so the race began top of Flanna hill we raced our machines along Batley road past bottom of church hill and all the way up to babes in the wood I beat him there and I beat him back an all Alan never said much he said nothing in fact apart from well done he was hurt though that was obvious cos ego played a massive part in things as a 17-year-old kid I was no *different and neither was Alan he had been the daddy up until me getting mine so things changed after that I never bragged I had a fast bike I did not need to and besides Angie loved it cos it meant she didn't mind riding back of my DT she never really like being on back of my DT but this was a whole new ball game finally it felt nice to be seen riding a shiny showroom condition Marlborough LC I rode it with pride and looked after it with pride an all every weekend stripped the head off and decoked the piston etc. lubed the chain and greased the cables.*

All I needed now was the summer to come along the following year and it did that Christmas we all rode into the Phoenix youth club and sat around in there few games of table tennis and what have yh and that was where folk would find us on the really cold Thursday nights the Phoenix was at the time the hub of the community and had been since way back in 78 as an 11-year-old boy so many happy times were spent in that old building on corner of Flanshaw lane and the hosts were great too Bob And Sheila as usual by now myself and the lads had bought the new style cotton racing jackets from sprint motorcycles on Donny rd. they had them hung up in the window mine was red it pretty much matched my bike and added to the pose factor I guess bloody warm too they were Angie had one too as did most the gang and by now the new year the new ridings had opened in wakey I'll never forget walking in there once to meet up with everyone and as I looked up towards the top balcony a line of colour greeted my eyes as all the gang was on the top leaning over the barriers just a sea of red blue white jackets we were finally a proper gang which had evolved from thugs on wall to proud bikers we all felt part of something and it felt at the time it would last forever only thing that could and would stop us would be growing up and no way did any of us want any of that yes that bike gang will go down in Flanshaw folk lore it really was that good and so xmas 84 came and went shops were shut again over the break from work so I bought my old holburn rolling baccy in advance supply's to get me over the break cos shops were always shut right into and some, not all opened again January 2nd so after a great xmas eating my head off at home I landed in 1985

That summer was up there in my memories nearly as good as 1976 it was our first summer together as the flanshaw bike gang and we wasted no time to have parties on side of the beck I once called for Neil and I remarked: "what's that under your jacket"? he just looked at me and smiled and we pull up the top of the hill I crogged him up there cos his bike was off the road and we pull up I jumps off the bike and sat on the bench with my girlfriend Angie and rest of gang so Neil pulls out this carrier from under his jacket and shouts top of his voice " sausages sausages" laughing as he said it we all look at him puzzled faces the lasses laughing their heads off and us all thinking like wot the hell ? and he says "sod this let's have a barby? come on down by beck " and so we did cos it was different and we like different we liked random we liked craziness and we lived for the next buzz and so off we scarpered home to raid our mums fridges we took burgers sausages hot dogs but we bought bread round at flanshaw shops and the beer of course and everyone had a great time Kev Alans Brother brought along his ghetto blaster and we blasted out theme songs from the wanderers film on it walk like a man being the most popular we made the fire and we sat around telling stories it soon got onto ghost stories so we all decided to stagger up to Saint Paul's churchyard for laugh oh I forgot to mention too we had a new kid in the gang called Talcy and he was as strange as they come or should I say cheekily ? because the night we met him we were all on the bench and he comes flying past forking us as he did and we were all wondering who the hell is that? so anyway he burned past us a few times and finally stopped taking off his helmet walked over to us and randomly shouts "hi I'm Talcy and I think your all tossers" we all just seemed to look at each other gobsmacked speechless.

So then He walks back to his bike kicks it over and speeds off he was riding a white RD LC 80 nippy little bugger it was an all, we all sat there thinking who the hell was that? anyway he comes back again jumps off his bike and offers me a smoke, so back to churchyard then so we gets to top of church hill and Talcy says here before you go in there let me show you something so he pulls out his lighter unscrews his petrol tanks picks up a bit of paper off the floor lights it at this point we had already backed off over a mile looking at one another what the hell is he doing? The mad hatter and as we realized what his intentions where we ran in all directions he lit the paper and threw it inside his tank the world stopped for me for a few seconds and I Held my breath nowt happened it could have and that was Talcy for you, always in the thick of things and random as hell a practical joker we welcomed him into our fold and he fitted in just perfectly. Meanwhile in the Churchyard and feeling a bit drunk big gang of us walks up and down the pavement between the graves me and Neil decided to play our own practical joke and we let Talc in on our plan so me and Neil grabs some old newspaper from the litter bin by the holy water tap and sneaks off we saw a freshly dug grave and decided to jump down it then cover ourselves over with the wooden planks we asked Talcy to fetch all lasses over and our plan went perfectly Talcy got them all close up and stood over the grave there was so many of us no one missed us and we waited and waited I just remember it was freezing down that hole even though it was a warm summers evening

And we picked our moment perfect as Talcy pulled across the planks of wood asking the lasses "wonder what's under there like"? and as he said this we lit the paper and made groaning noises! Never saw so many bodies run in all directions or hear as many screams basically looked like and sounded like a scene from the Evil Dead. Happy days and that was pretty much our Flanna gang full of crazy random stunts like that, we were like the gang on the video the Wanderers we were dropouts and outsiders hated and despised us I think mostly because we were noisy buggers as we pretty much made Flanshaw hill and those s bends our race track racing up and down it most nights but we were hated too I guess because we were young stupid naïve kids having fun growing up together making mistakes falling out drinking smoking even too early morning rides to Scarborough on those warm summer evenings of 1985 and we pretty much saw out that summer doing most the things explained above . Happy times, so one day we were all sat on the bench and suddenly out of nowhere came Alan on this brand-new Machine it was a Suzuki RG 125 Gamma the new generation of learner bikes at the time it was smaller than my LC anyway Alan pulls up and to be honest we were mostly Yamaha boys in our gang so anything other than one of these were looked upon with ridicule

Now I'm not saying it wasn't a nice bike because it was but my god it looked more like an Airfix model than a bike. For a start, you could not see any chrome or even the engine it was all hidden away with a full fairing I once had a ride on it and got blown all over place, not the bike for me I'm afraid and I remember everyone debating whether it would match or even beat my LC as it was modern it was lighter than mine and sleeker I must admit I was a bit worried myself , and after much-heated debate me and Alan decided to please the masses so after a bit of banter we set off up to mad mile to settle a score we crawled up there at snales pace the adrenalin was rushing as we banked left onto the mad mile suddenly we both open up he shot off quite quickly and got ahead of me this seemed top last ages then suddenly I hit 5.800 rpm and my Lc's powerband kicked in the only way to describe the powerband is that of a horse suddenly breaking into a gallop and I gained ground suddenly he was in my sights no words in the world can explain the Adrenalin rush of racing someone especially when your young and dumb as I was your pride and joy your bike your reputation all on the line so by now I'm gaining ground the powerband suddenly kicked in from nowhere, I never even knew it had a second one but it did then again I had never ridden my bike as hard as this before either so a second powerband kicks in and I pass him just as we approach the roundabout at chickenly and as I had done a bike course I knew and understood race lines how to get around a bend as quickly and smoothly as possible and that is what I did on that roundabout Kenny Roberts would have been proud I exited it at speed and raced off well ahead I rode past flanshaw hotel and saw the gang top of the hill my moment had arrived my bike and my reputation intact.

So that was that I thought but how wrong was I everyone wanted another race this time between me and Daz and as we had Replica bikes it was in everyone's eyes the race of all races and so it happened me and Daz shook hands mounted our machines and off we went to the mad mile again to firstly please the crowd but secondly to settle a score anyway to cut a long story short Daz beat me by a mile there and back and obviously his machine was more powerful plus he was short and lightweight too but it was the race everyone wanted no one was that surprised I would get beat cos it really was a fined tuned machine and personally I was not to bothered either after al it was an LC and as the year drew close to its end that was pretty much it back on the personal front me and Angie found ourselves more at home watching the soaps etc. and as it was really cold outside as the winter closed in I did not mind that sat cozy in front of me mums coal fire at Keswick Drive watching the soaps then not long after Angie got a job at a café in town and I used to meet her after work in there for a coffee then take her home on back of the bike to her house we seemed at this point to be getting close and I found my self-staying at

Angies much more than usual her mum was brilliant with me and she cooked a mean Yorkshire pud an all her dad Dave god rest his soul in heaven was too a really nice chap I'll never forget his smile it smiled with his eyes did Dave he had one of the nicest smiles I had ever seen.

I was always on my best behaviour when I was there used my manners mum had taught me to the max. I used to play pong donkey Kong and river raid on the little black and white portable that was parked in the corner of the kitchen with Angie's brother Glenn, while Angie would be sat watching the soaps with her mum in the room her dad was usually out on missions he did once take me to Bolton in his truck to empty an old pub over there it was at the time when they let Mira Hindley and Ian Brady out of the nick and took them over Saddleworth moor we drove past the snake pass on m62 and saw helicopters in the sky and police cars all over shop it was like a military operation never saw them only on telly when we finally arrived home I had picked up a load of pint glasses ceramic ashtrays and beer mats took them home because we all smoked in our house never drank much but the glasses were well posh so I had to have them . And this really seemed the end of the road for our Flanshaw gang Neil ended up with Andrea Andrew Williams was with Michelle Lloyd was with Julie Talcy was with Tracey I was with Angie everyone seemed to get the dating bug, and like anything in life when it seems it will last forever it suddenly ends we still met up occasionally at the bench top of Flanshaw hill it was pretty much over once 1986 came around though. And I needed a new adventure I also needed more money because my mum had put our board and lodgings to make up for the shortfall with my sister moving out, also the bike was developing engine problems I was buying this that and everything crap I did not need really than one day after chatting with Gilly at work he was talking about the TA and told me how good it was to get out in fresh air keep fit and get well paid for it as it meant his wage could go on other things because the TA basically paid the bills and as with most things I didn't need much persuasion and Joined the TA on George street. Suddenly all the running around and climbing walls jumping obstacles again I felt like I was six years old again and running around on Flanshaw I also realized how unfit I had become riding that bike around all day I also felt really smart and proud walking through Flanshaw with my combats on every Tuesday and Thursday nights it also meant I did not have to watch the soaps with Angie anymore too which was a bonus

And after taking the oath to queen and country I embarked on new adventures it was about this time my brother Mick had moved out too so that left me and our Norm and my Mum the family was breaking up everyone was growing up and I realized this probably more than the others did so our Mick got himself a flat which at the time was back of the trinity ground I rode over there and helped him paint it all and gave it the once over with a few cans of magnolia it was a shared accommodation and students lived there but it suited my brother he was around like minded people and being Arty it gave him the peace and quiet he craved to pursue his interest in poetry and songs and playing guitar which he was heavily into at the time, yes me and our kid were pretty much chalk and cheese from the moment we born really, him being the quietest out the two of us but he had a knack our Mick as in whenever he opened his mouth he always had valid and interesting things to say very clever but also very shy, where as I was very extroverted and a tad loud but we respected our space me and our kid but even to this day we find it hard to be in the same room together for more than an hour. Even as kids my toys were different to his I had mousetrap he had chemistry set I had skateboard he had Guinness book of records and annuals of every kind encyclopedias and such I was into the sex pistols he was into the boomtown rats we even marked our territories out as kids in the bedroom, on my wall sex pistols rule ok on his wall Boomtown rats rule ok the differences between us were obvious even at an early age.

So back to the present day I found myself busier than I had been as a child in the good old days, I was working five days a week sometimes weekends also the drill hall on George Street took two nights a week up and once a month weekend camp, I had to attend all of these otherwise I would lose out on bonus the drill nights were great learning to match I was taught how to strip a rifle down blindfolded and put it all back together I fired machine guns and rifles run around fields climbed assault courses it was great fun what I didn't realize at the time though was the amount of time I was dedicating to it all my mates on the bench where few and far between the streets suddenly became quite walking that walk up to the drill hall I would occasionally pass them and they always shouted over

133

"never mind all that Rambo stuff Jon get yourself back on wall with the lads" and as much I wanted to do that I also realized I enjoyed what I was doing it didn't feel dead end I felt like I had a future in front of me and although I always joined in on their banter about me thinking I was John J Rambo I felt focused for the first time in my life then along came spring 1986 I was posted to Winchester for my basic training pass this and I became a fully qualified soldier, It was also the first time I had been away from home really apart from that week in cleethorpes with Tigger and his parents back in the 70s I spent two weeks down south away from Angie I have to admit it hurt me I missed her I missed being home I missed Flanshaw I felt at the time we were going places we had by this point been together nearly eighteen months now I practically lived round Angie's house at tea time, her mum and dad were probably sick of sight of me. She was also working full time now in that café in town owned by this old Scottish bloke who I didn't like if I'm honest seemed a tad creepy to me. as for myself I was working a full-time Job and was a part-time soldier on a weekend, the future looked rosy.

So fast forward to Winchester it was hell on earth down there as it was designed to be, me and my fellow soldiers from day one were broke down and made to feel incompetent we got picked at for pretty much everything we tried to do right every morning we awoke to the bugle player on the drill square and would rush out of our beds get the mop and bucket out and clean down 3 flights of stairs then onto our barracks floor make our beds and make that basically everything was in tip top shape before the corporal came along to inspect our handy work, Anyway this one time we had polished the floor so thorough we could see our faces in it same as our boots we could eat our dinner off it I swear , and besides we felt chuffed an all because as the days went by we got better at it and didn't have to do it all over again as the previous days , our corporal at the time a chap named Steve he was a Winchester lad and a right cocky sod he always carried a pick axe handle with him cos when the bugle player wasn't playing he would smash the door with it 5am crack of the sparrows fart as we called it back then and that woke us up pretty fast I can tell you that for nowt .

So, he walked through the barracks door, we all stood to attention at the end of our beds and he proceeded with his usual pacing up and down the room looking at us all cocky well everything was going fine and he was sitting his head in approval then it dawned on me as I saw him proceed to wipe top of our lockers with his index finger. I had not done mine! panic overtook me and I knew I had failed I knew this time anyway that I had let my buddies down and he did get to my locker and he did check it and he laughed he walks to the middle of the room and shouts right you have holey to blame for this and with that he dug his rubber soles into the floor and scratched a rubber line all along our shiny floor that was hard to take and I could not apologize enough to the lads but we were a team and we moved on from it, and most important of all we learned the lesson. and not the only one later that day we went on a ten-mile march and shoot over farmers ploughed fields by Stonehenge absolutely sapped the energy from you did a march and shoot, and before the run the corporal weighed all our Webbing it had to weigh twenty-nine pounds anyway we get to the end totally exhausted and shot we emptied our rifle magazines into the targets

We then did the assault course and got back to base we went in the utility room and washed our combats great you might say? Well yes, it was, only we had forgotten to label our uniforms it was a nightmare trying to find my size in a pile of the same clothing, about 35 combat uniforms with no names! Bloody nightmare, and there were many more silly things we would do along the way until we were told we were competent like I was pushed off the top diving board about 40 feet drop I was a bit scared but corporal didn't give me time to be as he strategically placed his size 9 on my ass,

On the final day when we passed out on the parade square it was the best feeling in the world we waved goodbye to all lads we had met from up and down the country and as our sergeant McClintock pulled on to the square in the wakey Minibus finally we made our way home I went there a boy and came home a man my mum said , and I remember walking over the road with a GPMG machine gun and bullet belt I really did feel like I was ten men like John J Rambo was in the movie, and after this adventure and soon as we had declared all our equipment back in the stores I headed off home,

Strange I thought no one on the bench no one down on the wall I called at Angies her mum answered but said she was out and this went on for rest of the day then as I'm walking to the shop for a pack of Regal Kings I heard from Talcy that she had left me for his mate and it gutted me but he said it right he felt for me too, which I found strange for him, and all of a sudden for probably the first time in my life I felt rejection I was only eighteen and Angie was only seventeen and its weird that at the time when you're in the moment you feel that you will last forever I was absolutely torn apart and that's it I never saw her again for years after but we were young we lived in the moment we were too naïve to understand it I used to sit on the wall a full qualified soldier reduced to a quivering wreck and it lasted a few months too that's how hard I took it at the time but a few Kestrel lagers later I was back on my feet and had moved on from her as sad as it was one thing being brought up on Flanshaw taught me and being an old Punk was to be tough when you had to and soft when you didn't and that's exactly what I did I had my pity party and I moved on. Our gang seemed to get back together for a while now Angie was out the way weirdly enough and we survived a few more months into the end of that summer 1986, My Job at Rawson's was safe but I left it, I tore up the past like a fool and looking back on it all my mind was elsewhere I had simply lost my focus I jacked in the TA too Losing Angie really was a kick in the teeth it threw me off the track for a while but the gang on the wall I had grown so close with they were always there for me , anyway I decided to pack in my job and go work with the lads at an engineering firm on Henry street at the time called Cranes well I thought it was going to be a blast a new start and I got to hang about with my pals but it all ended in tears and I lasted three months before me and a lad from our hang called Steve were sacked for bad timekeeping. But I didn't care I was not with Angie anymore and I had no one to answer to but myself and my mums board of course, but mum being mum she never complained she never made much fuss over it and that's how my mum rolled, once proverbial shit hit the fan she would simply smile shrug her shoulders pause a few seconds and say "you'll live" she said it ever since I was a kid when I broke my leg when I broke my arms three times and everything , and because she was not stressed then either was I, and I have my mum to thank for way I treat adversity these days she was and will always be my hero will Mum, and way she brought six of us up on her own and that is to be admired and I'll not forget and one of the reason's as well for my daughter Caitlen I wrote this book in the first place.

Chapter Fourteen

All Good Things Come to An End

Christmas came and I went out with the 'lads once again I met up with some old mates from Rawson's for a sesh in town as the gang all had girlfriends at this point so they acted boring to be quite honest I couldn't wait to see the year out because although it had brought me luck and also transformed me from a boy to a man, on the other hand, it had also destroyed my dreams and that was that and the new year came along fresh year fresh start still on the dole though and had to sell my treasured Marlborough bike that was so hard to do I tell yeah it was like losing my girlfriend Angie all over again but this year had something much bigger in store for me big changes lay ahead bigger than anything I had just been through my brother Steve had been with his girlfriend a few years now one day he came over to our house and sat our norm down he explained that he was selling up both him and his girlfriend and their plan was to buy a bungalow on outskirts of Wakefield and he asked our Norm if he wanted to buy his house on Eastmoor .

Our kid agreed and I that was that really it took a few months for it all to go through and it was not long after that I realized once our kid moved out that would leave me and my mum we had a three-bedroom house I kind of knew what was coming although mum held on to me and her home as long as she could but even mum could not get us out of this one , the world was changing the family grown up everyone were suddenly doing their own thing now and we were no longer kids anymore,

My heart sunk as mum sat me down and showed me a letter from council asking us politely to vacate the property, as they had offered my mum a flat and I had no alternative but to move on to Eastmoor with my brother Thirteen happy years were coming to a close in my life my whole childhood the person I am today is all down to that street the friends I met along the way and that house I grew up in the place I still call home to this day it made me, it broke me I had laughed a lot in it I had cried a lot in it I had experienced love and lost love in it too , but the journey the adventures I had tasted I I can never forget unfortunately had reached its destination and it was a sad day the day I moved out of there .

Cried? yes, I did I cried like a baby that first night in my new bedroom on Eastmoor but such is life. Besides I was now the ripe old age of twenty no longer in a job lost my girlfriend it just seemed looking back on it all these things had to end when I left that old street, in order for me to discover new adventures. Mum went with the flow she took it much easier than I ever did , I think she was kind of happy in a way as the flat she moved into is a very cosy comfortable home, has been for years for her, besides why shouldn't she have felt a sense of relief and a job well done ,after all she had brought all of us up by herself and made plenty of sacrifices for us along the way, she still lives in that flat to this day , she has outlived all her friends on her street many times over and I guess the only downside is by doing so and growing old gracefully as mum has, you naturally lose a lot of people and good friends in your life and she has ,but she rides the storm she always had, but she's in a comfortable place today and for that I am relieved everything has worked out just fine for her .

As for me? well, many more adventures lay ahead for me after I moved off that magical old street, A part two maybe? Who knows eh?
Well as my Flanshaw tale draws to a close I want to thank you all for your support and encouragement throughout the time of writing this, it has given me a sense of pride again, something over the years I did seem to have lost a bit of, and I have only you the reader to thank for sticking with me and encouraging me to keep it going, when at times all I wanted to do was throw in the towel.
Well, that's it! for now, I will say goodbye until the next one. Thank you all for reading my Flanshaw Tale.

Printed in Great Britain
by Amazon